RESTAURANT MANAGEMENT

RESTAURANT MANAGEMENT

V.K. Gupta
Principal
Greenfields College of Catering
& Hotel Management,
Hyderabad

AMAN PUBLICATIONS
NEW DELHI

Published by
Rajiv Jain for Aman Publications
LG-4A, Ganpati Bhawan,
4675-B/21, Ansari Road,
Darya Ganj, Delhi - 110002
PH: 23255012, 23282127
E-mail: sshjbs@yahoo.com

Edition : 2020

Rs.650/-

ISBN–81–8204–038-8

SOLE DISTRIBUTOR
JINDAL BOOK SERVICES
LG-4A, Ganpati Bhawan,
4675-B/21, Ansari Road,
Darya Ganj, Delhi - 110002

Laser Typesetting by:
APCON, Delhi,
Ph: 39542551, 9811571141

Printed by:
Tarun Offset, Delhi, India

CONTENTS

PREFACE

Restaurants are establishments that serve prepared food and beverages to be consumed on the premises. They are sometimes a feature of a larger complex, typically a hotel, where the dining amenities are provided for the convenience of the residents and, of course, for the hotel to maximise their potential revenue.

Restaurants range from unpretentious lunching or dining places catering to people working nearby, with simple food served in simple settings at low prices, to expensive establishments serving refined food and wines in a formal setting. In the former case, customers usually wear casual clothing. In the latter case, depending on culture and local traditions, customers might wear semi-casual, semi-formal, or even in rare cases formal wear. Restaurants often specialise in certain types of food or present a certain unifying, and often entertaining, theme. For example, there are seafood restaurants, vegetarian restaurants or ethnic restaurants.

This book deals with various facets of restaurant management with special focus on service quality. It could be utilised by anyone and everyone related to the field of restaurant management, right to the field of hospitality management, right from students, teachers, researchers, practitioners to business persons and related professionals.

1

Introduction to Restaurant Management

A restaurant is an establishment that serves prepared food and beverages to be consumed on the premises. The term covers a multiplicity of venues and a diversity of styles of cuisine. Restaurants are sometimes a feature of a larger complex, typically a hotel, where the dining amenities are provided for the convenience of the residents and, of course, for the hotel to maximise their potential revenue. Such restaurants are often also open to non-residents.

The term *restaurant* (from the French *restaurer*, to restore) first appeared in the 16th century, meaning "a food which restores", and referred specifically to a rich, highly flavoured soup. According to the Guinness Book of Records, the Sobrino de Botin in Madrid, Spain is the oldest restaurant in existence today. It opened in 1725.

The modern sense of the word was born around 1765 when a Parisian soup-seller named Boulanger opened his establishment. The first restaurant in the form that became standard (customers sitting down with individual portions at individual tables, selecting food from menus, during fixed opening hours) was the *Grand Taverne de Londres*, founded in 1782 by a man named Beauvilliers. Whilst inns and taverns were known from antiquity, these were establishments aimed at travellers, and in general locals would rarely eat there.

The restaurant became established in France after the French Revolution broke up catering guilds and forced the aristocracy to flee, leaving a retinue of servants with the skills to cook excellent food; whilst at the same time numerous provincials arrived in Paris with no family to cook for them. Restaurants were the means by which these two could be brought together — and the French tradition of dining out was born. In this period the star chef Auguste Escoffier, often credited with founding classic French cuisine, flourished, becoming known as the "Cook of Kings and the King of Cooks."

Restaurants then spread rapidly across the world, with the first in the United States (*Jullien's Restarator*) opening in Boston in 1794. Most however continued on the standard approach (*Service à la française*) of providing a shared meal on the table to which customers would then help themselves, something which encouraged them to eat rather quickly. The modern formal style of dining, where customers are given a plate with the food already arranged on it, is known as *Service à la russe*, as it is said to have been introduced to France by the Russian Prince Kurakin in the 1810s, from where it spread rapidly to England and beyond.

Types of Restaurant

Brasserie, Bistro, Pub

In France, a brasserie is a café doubling as a restaurant and serving single dishes and other meals in a relaxed setting. A bistro is a familiar name for a café serving moderately priced simple meals in an unpretentious setting, especially in Paris; bistros have become increasingly popular with tourists. Mainly in the UK and other countries influenced by British culture, the pub (short for public house) today serves a similar dual menu, offering beer and other alcohol along with basic food fare. Traditionally, pubs were primarily drinking establishments, whereas the modern pub business relies on food as well, to the point where so-called gastropubs are known for their high-quality "pub food".

Dining Car

A dining car (restaurant car) or diner (but not "diner car," except in uninformed parlance) is a railroad passenger car that serves meals on a train in the manner of a full-service, sit-down restaurant. It is distinct from other types of railroad food-service cars that do not duplicate the full-service restaurant experience, principally cars of various types in which one purchases food from a walk-up counter to be consumed either within the car or elsewhere in the train. While dining cars are less common today than they were in the past, they still play a significant role in passenger railroading, especially on medium- and long-distance trains.

Fast Food Restaurants

In the U.S., fast-food restaurants and take-outs have become so widespread that the traditional standard type is now sometimes referred to as a sit-down restaurant (a retronym). A common feature of fast food restaurants is a lack of cutlery or crockery, the customer is expected to eat the food directly from the disposable container it was served in using their hands.

There are various types of fast-food restaurant:

— one collects food from a counter and pays, then sits down and starts eating (self-service restaurant); sub-varieties:

— one collects ready portions
— one serves oneself from containers
— one is served at the counter
— a special procedure is that one first pays at the cash desk, collects a ticket and then goes to the food counter, where one gets the food in exchange for the ticket
— one orders at the counter; after preparation the food is brought to one's table; paying may be on ordering or after eating.

Family Style

"Family style", or sometimes called *table d'hôte* ("host's table") in France, are restaurants that have a fixed menu and fixed price, usually with dinners seated at a communal table such as on bench seats. More common in the 19th and early 20th century, they can still be found in rural communities, or as theme restaurants, or in vacation lodges. There is no menu to choose from, rather food is brought out in courses, usually with communal serving dishes, like at a family meal. Typical examples can include crab-houses, German-style beer halls, BBQ restaurants, hunting/fishing lodges. Some normal restaurants will mix elements of family style, such as a table salad or bread bowl that is included as part of the meal.

Restaurant Guides

Restaurant guides list the best places to eat. One of the most famous of these, in Western Europe, is the Michelin series of guides which accord from 1 to 3 stars to restaurants they perceive to be of high culinary merit. Restaurants with stars in the Michelin guide are formal, expensive establishments; in general the more stars awarded, the higher the prices. In the United States, the

Mobil Travel Guides and the AAA rate restaurants on a similar 1 to 5 star (Mobil) or Diamond (AAA) scale. Three, four, and five star/diamond ratings are roughly equivalent to the Michelin one, two, and three star ratings while one and two star ratings typically indicate more casual places to eat. In 2005, Michelin released a New York City guide, its first for the United States. The popular Zagat Survey compiles individuals' comments about restaurants but does not pass an "official" critical assessment.

The largest restaurant and menu guide is MenuPix.com. They offer over 15,000 restaurant menus in cities such as New York, Los Angeles, Boston, DC and San Francisco. Nearly all major American newspapers employ restaurant critics and publish online dining guides for the cities they serve. American newspaper restaurant critics typically visit dining establishments anonymously and return several times so as to sample the entire menu. Newspaper restaurant guides, therefore, tend to provide the most thorough coverage of various cities' dining options.

Economics of Restaurants

In economics, restaurants are the end of the supply chain in the foodservice industry. There is usually much competition in most cities since barriers to entry are relatively low, which means that for most restaurants, it is hard to make a profit. In most First World industrialized countries, restaurants are heavily regulated to ensure the health and safety of the customers. The typical restaurant owner faces many obstacles to success, including raising initial capital, finding competent and skilled labour, maintaining consistent and excellent food quality, maintaining high standards of safety, and the constant hassle of minimising potential liability for any food poisoning or accidents that may occur. Additionally, when economic conditions change—for example an increase in gasoline prices—households typically spend less on dining out.

The restaurant industry includes many 'different types of facilities and markets. Social and economic trends have emerged to shape the restaurant industry. The most profound trend is the working woman. With a larger income, women view restaurants not only as an affordable way to dine, but also as a convenience for themselves and their family. Restaurants provide an alternative to the added stress of arriving home from the office and dropping everything to cook the family's evening meal. The increase in household incomes has created a desire and convenience for people to spend time dining away from home or ordering takeout meals. The association cites households with a pretax income of $30,000 or more spends a larger amount of time dining out.

In short, the increase in working women has created a larger household income in which people can afford to eat away from home. The mere convenience of avoiding a night of cooking over the stove after a long day at the office is enticing to many women and their families. This trend is expected to remain long-term as people's lives continue on a fast-paced schedule. Whether it's driving a son or daughter to a school function or staying late at the office, sitting down at home for a meal with the entire family is hard to come by. From a promotional products perspective, understanding the driving forces behind the changes in the restaurant industry will enable eatery owners to properly target the audience they decide to pursue.

Segments of Restaurant Industry

The restaurant industry has two distinct audience segments: full- and limited-service operations. Both segments attract a certain clientele as well as various promotional products.

Full-Service Segment of Restaurant Industry

The full-service segment of the restaurant industry can be categorised as sit-down restaurants that cater to the customer with a sense of personal attention. For example, an Italian restaurant with a hostess, a choice of wines and Italian music playing softly in the background is a full-service experience. Many full-service restaurants are competing for customers, not only in the full-service market, but with the fast-food or limited-service segment of the industry as well.

Full-service restaurants are generally categorised in terms of price, menu, or atmosphere.

— *Price*: When the focus is on price, restaurants can be categorised as luxury, highpriced, mid-priced, or low-priced establishments.

— *Menu*: Restaurants such as steak houses and seafood restaurants are full service restaurants defined in terms of menu. For example, Outback Steakhouse specialises in beef; Red Lobster features shrimp, crab, and lobster on its menu.

— *Atmosphere*: Some restaurants are known primarily for their atmosphere that is, for their unique architecture, decor, and / or setting. Show business and sports motifs-currently very fashionable in the industry-provide themes for a growing number of popular restaurants. The Hard Rock Cafe chain, which started in London and now has restaurants in major cities around the world, features Elvis Presley, the Beatles, and other rock-star music memorabilia. Other categories.

Full-service restaurants can be categorised in other ways besides price, menu, or atmosphere. For example, there are dinner houses. Dinner houses are distinguishable by their combination of decor, informal atmosphere, and eclectic menus that draw from ethnic and traditional offerings. Family restaurants serve breakfast, lunch, and dinner, offering traditional menu items. Their pricing falls between casual dinner houses and quick-service restaurants. A major source of revenue for some family restaurants-such as Cracker Barrel—is an on-site gift shop.

To compete against its market segment as well as other establishments, the fullservice restaurant prides itself on customer appreciation. To survive, full-service restaurants must have a loyal customer following. This is accomplished by offering unique menu choices and a creative atmosphere that will entice the customer not only to return, but also to inform his or her acquaintances of the establishment. The biggest challenge for full-service operators is to attract customers, then maintain their loyalty. The 90s brought the theme restaurants. These include restaurants catering to music, movies, sports or environmental enthusiasts. Many theme establishments have the advertising and physical appearance to draw customers from all walks of life. Many are tourists who want an opportunity to view memorabilia and catch a glimpse of the creative interior that mirrors the establishment's theme.

Most full-service restaurants, especially theme establishments, will include logoed merchandise as a method of advertising. Customers will find T-shirts and a host of other items with a restaurant's logo on them. These items play an important role in earning customer loyalty and promoting the name of the establishment. Distributors have an advantage servicing the restaurant industry because they simply need to walk inside an establishment to get a hint of its décor and customer base, thus receiving a better idea as to what promotional products would be most appealing to the customers. On the other end of the scale, limited-service restaurants cater to a much fasterpaced clientele.

With corporate downsizing, employees are working longer hours and having meals ordered at the workplace. Longer hours and lack of time have transformed family mealtime into "home meal replacement." Fast-food restaurants and delis offer convenient alternatives to people on the go. The drive-up window has replaced the dining room in many limited-service establishments. In US, the National Restaurant Association states that nearly 30 percent of all retail establishments are eating and drinking places. Both the retail and bookstore markets are incorporating food services as a marketing tool to keep customers in the stores longer.

The grocery stores already have used food to entice its customers to stay and shop; however, many customers will purchase a carryout meal to avoid preparing a meal when they get home. Gasoline convenience stores are growing tremendously because of the possibility for additional revenue from drivers traveling on a trip or returning home from work. Many are building in residential areas in order to be easily accessible to nearby residents. The limited-service segment opens many doors to food-on-the-go suppliers who are interested in testing unique products specifically designed for the customer on the move. With intense competition between limited-service establishments, owners must rely on creative ideas to separate themselves from the rest of the competition.

For example, a product that fits in the automobile to serve as a reminder to visit a convenience store for gasoline and sandwiches is a marketing tool appropriate for people whose car has taken the place of the kitchen table. With thousands of restaurants to choose from, distributors must understand the establishment, its clientele and the competition to offer promotional products that will make a lasting impact. Whether it is full- or limited-service establishments, there are differences in the needs of restaurants within these segments. What works for the Italian restaurant may not work for the Mexican restaurant down the street.

Promotional products are heavily based on customer demand or the usefulness of the product for the market's customers. Two full-service restaurants that have survived the times and made a lasting name for themselves both nationally and worldwide are Ithaca, New York-based Moosewood Restaurant and Driftwood, Texas-based The Salt Lick. Despite outside competition and slow seasons, both restaurants have retained customer loyalty by listening to the needs of its customers. The Moosewood Restaurant is a vegetarian restaurant established in 1973 at a time when people were asking themselves if they could eat just vegetables. Situated in the same spot in Ithaca, New York, the restaurant has undergone several design changes over the years.

What is interesting about the successes of the Moosewood Restaurant and The Salt Lick is the creative uses of cookbooks and barbecue sauce to promote the restaurant on a grand scale. While it may not have been apparent to the establishments at the time, the cookbooks and sauce were innovative promotional products that continue to generate revenue for the restaurants more than 20 years after their inception. Several years later, both establishments have incorporated common-day promotional items to promote themselves.

Limited-Service Restaurant

It is for this segment of the population that limited-service restaurants were created. Whether it is a fast-food chain, coffeehouse or stop-and-go, the limitedservice establishment is providing customers with a demanding convenience. In US, the National Restaurant Association indicates that one out of five takeout food consumers is a daily user. Those customers represent half of all takeout occasions. Major growth in quick-service restaurants continues to come from hamburger chains as well as chicken, sandwich, and Mexican-food chains. Much of the growth is outside the United States. The type or number of menu items alone does. not determine the winners. A commitment to good service and providing nutritional menu choices has taken center stage.

McDonald's now guarantees hot food; fast, friendly service; and double-check drive-thru accuracy. A survey of 27 restaurant chains-including 19 quick-service chains-with 50,000 outlets found that at least three-quarters of them offered menu choices for health-conscious consumers. Examples included low-fat milk, skinless chicken, and reduced or low-calorie salad dressing. Nine out of ten chains said they used vegetable fats instead of animal fats for frying. While a limited-service establishment may not have all the personal touches of a full-service restaurant, there is a loyalty among limited-service customers that promotional products can reach.

With intense competition emerging between limitedservice establishments, it is becoming increasingly important to maintain a loyal customer base. An important method of accomplishing that is incorporating promotional products into the customers' orders. For fast-food restaurants such as McDonald's and Burger King, children have enjoyed kid's meals that include plastic toys depicting the establishment's mascots. Coffeehouses have used creative ideas such as cooking a muffin in a logoed coffee mug that the customer keeps for refills during repeat visits.

Other limited-service establishments include logoed T-shirts, matchbooks, coasters, magnets and buttons.

The limited-service market has many opportunities for promotional products. The National Restaurant Association notes that in an average month 78 percent of U.S. households use some form of carryout or delivery. It is obvious that the limitedservice market has a large audience that can be reached via promotional products. For example, ast-food restaurants have been offering logoed glasses and toys to customers for many years. Promotional products are an inexpensive medium that limited-service establishments can utilise to promote their name and logo to the public. The full-service market is custom-oriented; therefore, it is essential that distributors create a promotion that leaves a sense of appreciation in the customer. Full-service establishments want and need customers to return and a well-crafted promotional product could be the difference between a high turnover or a loyal customer base.

The limited-service market works in a similar manner. Although limited service establishments need customers, the focus is to create name and logo recognition to a mass audience. With millions of people who enjoy hamburgers, limited-service operators must separate themselves from the rest of the competition that sells hamburgers. To accomplish this, promotional products with a relatively low cost and function can create long-term exposure to a large audience.

Lodging Food Service Operations

Food service outlets in lodging operations range from gourmet restaurants to coffee shops and even quick-service outlets. Lodging food service sales are tremendous.

— *Transportation Market*. Travellers eat at highway stops; on airplanes, ships, and trains; at airport terminals and train stations; and at other facilities in the transportation market-a market that enjoys about $3.7 billion in sales each year. Cruise lines put a great deal of emphasis on their food service. Industry surveys cite the food served shipboard as one of the top reasons for taking a cruise and selecting a specific line. Royal Caribbean International's 142,000-ton Voyager of the Seas carries 3,114 passengers and a crew of 1,181; fully 30 percent of the crew works in the kitchen. Royal Caribbean has won numerous international awards for its food. Food service in airports and train terminals is often provided by restaurants—frequently limited-menu restaurants-and contract food companies such as ARAMARK that bid for the opportunity to sell food in the terminals.

Many airlines today are trying to differentiate themselves, at least on routes they share with several competing airlines, by serving more distinctive food in business and first-class sections, using fresh food instead of frozen items when possible. Even the selection of wines available on board has been greatly upgraded in some instances. Although airline passenger traffic is strong, growth in food and drink sales has reached a plateau, in part because food service on many flights has been cut back due to the growing popularity of no-frills air carriers such as Southwest and Midway.

Recreational Market. The recreational market includes food service facilities located at sports arenas, stadiums, racetracks, movie theaters, bowling alleys, amusement parks, municipal convention centers, and other attractions. All together, this is an $11.7 billion market. In many cases, recreational-market food service facilities are concessions run by contract food companies.

— *Business and Industry Market*. The business and industry market consists of nonfood service businesses that offer on-site food service to their employees. Most businesses that provide employee meals use contract food companies such as Sodexho and ARAMARK. At Pacific Bell in San Ramon, California, ARAMARK offers food service to 8,500 employees. A number of food stations serve such fare as Asian and Mexican dishes, sandwiches, salads, pizza, pasta, desserts, and specialty drinks called "smoothies."

— *Educational Market*. One of the biggest changes in college food service programmes has been the gradual shift from mandated meal plans to a la carte operations. Due in part to this shift, many college food service operators have become revenue producers instead of revenue consumers for their colleges. Another change in college food service programmes has come about because an increasing number of nontraditional students are going to college today. Therefore, dining directors have had to change their food service programmes to accommodate preferences that are somewhat different from those of the typical 18-year-old.

— *Health Care Market*. The health care market consists of three principal segments: hospitals and other medical centers, nursing homes, and retirement communities (including congregate food sites-community-sponsored meal centers for senior citizens). Many experts believe that there is enormous potential for food service management companies in the health care market. This can be attributed to a combination of factorsrapidly changing life-styles, an aging population, skyrocketing medical costs, restricted federal funds, and a lack of family support systems. Most health care facilities run their own food service departments, some of which can be quite extensive.

Many hospitals operate vending machines, visitor coffee shops, employee cafeterias, special dining facilities for doctors, day-care food programmes for employees' children, regular patient food programmes, and special patient food programmes that can include gourmet meals (with accompanying wines) served in patient rooms.

— *Retail Market*. Two major trends in food service have surfaced in recent years. The first is the increasing tendency of Americans to eat food prepared outside of the home, as evidenced by the dramatic growth in restaurant food sales. The second trend, which is developing even more rapidly, is the growth in the take-out and delivery segment of the market. It is clear that Americans are cooking less. It is also clear that there is a growing inclination to buy food prepared outside the home and bring it home to consume it. This last development is in line with marketing trends in other areas such as home electronics and furniture, where research has shown that, at an increasing rate, people use their homes as recreational and entertainment centers.

Some industry observers expect the average supermarket to increase in size from its present 30,000-50,000 square feet to 200,000 square feet (2,790-4,650 square meters to 18,600 square meters). Much of that space will be devoted to precooked take-out dishes and sitdown food service areas. Many supermarkets already offer take-out salad bars in addition to their traditional deli sections. Using ovens in their bakeries, many of today's supermarkets are preparing a complete line of food products for their small in-store restaurants and cafeterias.

Supermarket research shows that supermarket produce is perceived to be fresher than that sold in most restaurants. Some supermarkets are taking advantage of this perception by selling a wide range of freshly prepared salad and vegetable dishes. Some have hired chefs to work in open kitchens so that customers can actually see that dishes are prepared with fresh-not frozen-ingredients. Another supermarket food service trend is the growth of food courts. Supermarket chains are installing food courts (similar to those found in shopping malls) in hopes of winning back some of the food dollars they have lost to restaurants.

Correctional institutions often have a hard time attracting and retaining food service staff because they cannot offer much professional career growth. However, the unique challenge they do offer can be attractive to some people. A prison must offer a cyclical menu that is not overly repetitive and has the flexibility to meet special religious and medical dietary needs, while still offering a bit of creativity in both preparation and presentation. Theft is another problem encountered by prison food service systems. Stringent controls must be used. Food costs are a further constraint on operations. Correctional institutions often have limited budgets for food service; economies of scale can thus make a substantial difference in the type and variety of food that can be offered to inmates.

Contract food management companies offer numerous careers in restaurant management. Many contractors recruit on college campuses. As increasing numbers of consumers want to either dine out or take prepared food home, the number of food-service operations has skyrocketed from 155,000 about 25 years ago to nearly 800,000 today. But there's still room in the market for your food-service business. Shifting demographics and changing lifestyles are driving the surge in food-service businesses. Busy consumers don't have the time or inclination to cook. They want the flavor of fresh bread without the hassle of baking. They want tasty, nutritious meals without dishes to wash.

In fact, the rise in popularity of to-go operations underscores some clear trends in the food-service industry. More and more singles, working parents and elderly people are demanding greater convenience in buying their meals and are turning to operations that provide that convenience. Though the future looks bright for the food-service industry overall, there are no guarantees in this business. Even the most successful operators will tell you this isn't a "get rich quick" industry. It's more like a "work hard and make a living" industry. A hard reality is that many restaurants fail during their first year in business, frequently due to a lack of planning.

2

HOSPITALITY TRAINING

The hospitality industry is now considering putting much effort on education, and of the element to be paid attention is training and development. Rapid changing in environment must be dealt with 'freedom' of creativity, new approaches to staff, dealing with new technology conveying learning into their life at work, flexibility in organisation model, etc have become part of daily activities. All these issues are really now the driving forces for the hospitality industry to 'tap in' into the current environment. The question is how the whole 'perplexing' issues can be answered in today's business life.

The hospitality industry ought to rely on model of strategic business management to accelerate the sensitivity of growing expectations from customers. The model below attempts to accommodate the variety of issues in today's environment as part of the strategic model. The hospitality industry must realise that designing a model of the strategic management ought to be looking at the wide range of components that might be affecting its performance. One of the main thing should be addressed is the dynamic environment.

All aspects of factors beyond the industry have put in place before proceeding to the plan. Identifying the variety of environment can be valuable for both the company and its clients. No longer 'gambling' or 'intuitive' or 'personal feelings' recommendation to establish the business objectives. One thing should be done is compiling significant information of existing market and trying to break them down into scale of priorities. One of the difficulties facing the hospitality industry these days is hiring the skilled person(s) to synthesise relevant information. The critical point here is the hospitality industry must be able to accommodate its current resources and be persistent about where we want to go.

A lot of experts argue that a strategic management model can only be applied to anticipate the changing environment. Unfortunately, this is not right. What managers should do is developing the model and 'engineering' the environment to fit with the proposed model. One possible method is to create a market that attracts customers to come, and ensure they will come back again. Price and quality could have been used as the tools to create new opportunities. The model above might be used to put some ideas to fix the old paradigm of 'anticipating' and 'adjusting' model and move to a 'dynamic' model that can be flexible in current and future environment. By (always) related back to your vision and strategic objectives, the hospitality industry has to catch up with future environment.

The problem within the hospitality industry is having a lack of vision, and the industry has only long-term strategic plans. What happens with the environment is it changes rapidly. Therefore, the hospitality industry must make and develop its strategic model to speed up its role of current and future environment. This means that the hospitality industry ought to focus primarily upon the needs of all employees be reoriented to changing conditions. The human aspects should be given more attention in today's environment. The model above depicted that understanding and underlying the importance of the strategic business objectives in line with corporate vision should be transformed into 'transferable manner' that employees might able to follow them up. Thus, it certainly requires management's support (i. e. motivation, reinforcement, reward and recognition). The central focus on this model is the hospitality industry must come up with strategies to achieve goals.

One possible strategy is to provide training and development that will lead to learning. Encouraging learning has become one of an international theme within the hospitality industry. There have been a lot of discussions in this matter whether an organisation should provide a specific training for a specific job or we offer a training package leading to multiskilling employees. This is "an old song in the new rhythms". The issue is not just be able to improve skills, but mastered in specific skills instead.

The main concern in the hospitality industry that customers demand professionalism on the jobs. If you are able to have different skills for different jobs, that's excellent. But, don't get too excited not being able to provide an outstanding service. The principle for the training process therefore getting new personnel and current staff to be able to play a role to the success of the organisation and then how the services or products of the organisation can contribute to society. The model indicates that the first step to be taken is induction programmes that are familiarising new employees to the organisation, their job, and the work unit.

During induction programmes, the hospitality industry tend to explain in details about the philosophy, culture, ways doing things, etc. This is quite right in one side to ensure that new employees are able to identify their current internal environment. However, this could be downgrading employees' expectation that may have different approaches about the existing atmosphere.

Instead of giving employees a bulk of big manuals to them, it would be better off for employees to adapt and be motivated that your contribution is really significant for our goals. One way to attain this is through socialisation that encourages employees to unite with current employees. Socialisation is the process through which new employees acquire the knowledge, skills, and attitudes that make them successful and to be integrated to the organisation and work department. Be ensure that the training programmes can and must encourage participants to learn, and managers have to motivate them to ensure that they will apply the new acquired skills in the worksite and learning transfer should be prioritised among managers.

Conducting evaluation would be the possible tool to find out whether training has been transferred or not is. Evaluation may be the least area to be considered and developed. Having 'smile sheets' is insufficient to render judgment about the effectiveness of your training activities, but it must involve the whole components (i. e. trainees' reaction, learning issues, behaviour and results) to find out how effective the programmes are. When the evaluation is completed, we are able to expect that the outcomes are positive and rewarding, both for those responsible for the programmes and for managers who will make decisions derived from their evaluation training programmes. The basic issue in the hospitality industry that a certain model must be developed to endeavor to lead in the future market.

The hospitality industry a picture of how necessary every step should be considered to execute the training programmes. Working on wrong assumptions may lead to design inappropriate training programmes that could create 'an undesired outcomes'. The current issues occurred in the workforce and attempt to 'tap in' into the model. The model into the current issues is the hospitality industry will be in favor position to compete in a world environment that in line with companies' vision and strategic objectives by designing the appropriate training programmes. More importantly, human relationships, information and willing to change will be seen as very imperative to attain desired outcomes. The model chosen attempts to accommodate the topical themes in the hospitality industry.

Training of Serving Customers

Training is about skills, knowledge and attitudes. Training is nothing more than providing you with the basic ability to provide uniformly high standards of service (how). An individual can demonstrate his or her ability (skills) to perform, then this individual does not require any more training. If someone possesses 'an adequate' skill, thus training is necessary to perform tasks 'according to standards'. To explore here is 'something' beyond the training programmes for persons who have had enough experience in the field. This may have been hidden for quiet long time. Again, in the hospitality industry, managers tend to seek someone who has a basic skill to perform (how well), and then from that basis, a new employee will be assigned to undertake further training to 'polish' with work standards (how). Thus, it appears that your past experience is 'only' working during recruitment and selection process.

Training programme is provided in line with the work standards. Most of the training managers have their own agenda to supply the industry with 'qualified staff' and this has to be done to achieve companies' vision and strategic objectives. However, there is one missing point here that the training programmes offered may far than staff's expectations. Experienced staff does not want any 'basic' skills anymore, but using his or her past experience to jump up to the next level, therefore, they require management development programmes.

Managers may argue that we 'expect' you to serve our guests according to the manuals and should follow literally. Everything has run smoothly and beautifully and there were not any mistakes. At the end of the day, managers will evaluate and give you a positive feedback. However, it was not the way it works at this hotel. The hotel expects you differently. It is only a matter of the 'right way' to service guests. The word 'expect' will sound explicitly. It can be seen that what happens to staff depends not just upon "how well" you serve, but also upon "how" you serve customers. "How well" you serve is related to individuals' skills, whereas "how" you serve customers is a matter of work procedures. Having had work experience is the good one and this may be useful to support your career progress. But, once again, if you have failed to execute the hotel work standards, it seemed unlikely for every staff to be promoted.

Originally, training programmes in the hospitality industry purpose:

— to support staff with basic skills required to perform tasks,
— to provide additional training (if it is required) to reduce the performance discrepancies, or to support for a new position,
— to supply employees to be able to carry the company's banner,
— to provide for staff with new acquired knowledge to achieve customers' expectation,

— to offer staff with 'appropriate' attitudes, and certain knowledge,

— lastly, managers expect staff to work uniformly high standards

Accountability of Training

Training is generally acknowledged as an important 'vehicle' for the hospitality industry. There have been a lot of facts, reviews and manuscripts to support this. Besides, generally known that training is also seen as an investment rather than just 'a regular programme' activity. Indeed, lots of researchers have acknowledged that the traditional view of training entails the following three components that can be useful to render the effectiveness of training programmes.

— A methodical assessment of training needs analysis to ensure that a training programme addresses issues and problems within the hospitality industry. A thorough needs analysis is used to determine where in the organisation training is needed, which employees require training, and what knowledge and or skills are required.

— Applying an appropriate training tools/methods to deliver content based on training needs analysis. The training methods depend upon the programme's objectives. Methods can be on the job training or off the job instruction. And each method is best utilized under particular conditions determined by the desired outcomes.

— A wide-ranging evaluation of the programme applying numerous different evaluation criteria and strategies to ascertain whether the desired outcomes have been achieved.

However, the problem appears to be narrowed on training specific features per se and it also seems that these components exclude such consideration of factors outside the training boundaries that could influence the effectiveness of any training effort. This outside factors could be individual and work environment that may also associate with training effectiveness. Therefore, training effectiveness, which is arguably, may not be able to stand firm with the instructional design and or contextual factors alone, but it may be caused by some 'unidentified factors' that tend to be 'left out' in every single discussion. Therefore, it is very interesting to explore what these 'unidentified factors' are.

Many questions have been arisen in educational literatures or empirical evidence that managers should ask how much money we spent on training in relation to employees' perceptions of the value of training. Although, it may be useful to know whether perceptions about training are in line with companies' financial commitments to this activity, it seems that the question has gone to the wrong address. The issue is not 'how much', or 'what employees' think', or 'what methods', but the issue is of what makes training effective.

Nevertheless, such an approach suggests that if desired results are not achieved with a considerable level of training expenditure, perceptions, or delivery issues, management will search for a reason for the failure and probably focusing on to the one of the three components above or could be all of them. Thus, such a failure may in fact have nothing to do with the training itself, because 'unidentified factors' may affect training effectiveness. The next thing is trying to find out the factors outside the training boundaries that appear to influence training effectiveness.

Evaluation of Training Programmes

Most hotels industry has invested their dollars on training. And each of hotel has a number of different ways to evaluate its training programmes and it depends upon the kind of training event, the aims of the training, the diversity of participants. But, still managers have doubt how to conduct evaluation. Issues such as who should be doing it, what purposes are, how to convince internal/ external customers, techniques. The most important aspect needs to be addressed prior to evaluate training programmes is that evaluation should be integrated into strategic business objectives.

There have been a lot of recipes of evaluating training programmes in very sophisticated explanations, arguments, charts and so forth but managers remain unclear about the purpose of it. Firstly, evaluation can supply valuable information on how the programme can be improved or terminated. It also can identify specific difficulties/ problems in the organisation, find out which training methods are effective, ascertain the significance of the programme in relations to the participants through improved KSAAE (knowledge, skills, ability, attitude and experience).

Indeed, evaluation can too be used to have a promotional agenda. In addition, evaluation is also of concern to achieve cost effectiveness. Finally, training programmes have to achieve the bottom line of the organisation objectives and this is where performance is linked to the organisational value or results. The "super model" of Kirkpatrick a four-stage evaluation model; reaction, learning, behaviour and results have been refined and revised. It seems straightforward to write about evaluation and to exhort others to carry out the task, but evaluation itself requires an integrated approach to ensure that training programmes are effective.

Evaluation appears to be a complex task, however, it depends upon how managers will do it. And again, every single task that relates to evaluation activities should link to the strategic business objectives. There is no doubt with current theories, models, charts about evaluation and they all seem practicable, but a nagging question is how we value training activities. This can be the reason that evaluating training programmes must relate to the strategic business objectives. Thinking about training evaluation for the hospitality industry requires a systematic approach to deal with. Indeed, it needs fully supports from managers to make certain that every single dollar spent on training programmes has been achieved.

In the hospitality industry, managers (usually) know what KSAAE their employees need to do their jobs, and then training them in those areas and at the end it will produce bottom line results. Training for front line employees is designed to ensure that they are able to undertake their tasks professionally and in the same manner. A hotel operator, for example, is given a job description before embarking to the actual workplace. Then, he/she will undergo a training programme that corresponds to the job.

Evaluation then seems relatively easy to conduct. If managers / supervisors/subordinates are willing to evaluate their staff, then the first thing they should do is addressing the performance back to the job description. Again, it is only a matter of can and can't do (my previous article) principle. Evaluation must go back to the strategic business objectives that convey mission and vision for the organisation. Another example would be training for front line staff to achieve an 'outstanding' customer service that correspond to the organisation's business objectives.

Training is then provided that supports the organisation's strategic objectives, but is also targeted to employee efforts. Evaluation then can be done through managers, peers or direct supervisors. These triangle sources of information then will make evaluation more valid. More importantly the using of customer service surveys will ensure the organisation that training produce the bottom lines.

Analysis of Training

Managers know exactly to come to a decision about whether or not to provide training for employees, and what type of training should be offered. Their decision has characteristically been based on the determination of training needs within organisations. TNA is very critical time for building links between training and results because the first part of decisions are made regarding what training will be given in organisations. The 'traditional' model of TNA which refers to three interrelated phases—needs analysis, execute and re-evaluation is workable in today's environment. The other three sub-aspects such as organisation, task and person analysis may be seen as very important to begin with and managers may have already done it within departments. The current model is okay but need to be supported by empirical evidence to ensure the model works.

Employees have to realise their ability to perform which relates to their daily activities and what sort of training to support his/her performance. The heads of departments have also to evaluate their staffs and find out the appropriate training for their employees if necessary. The most common way to do TNA is distributing a questionnaire. Every head of department has his/her own 'diary' about individuals' performance and the effective way to start of with TNA is checking a 'diary'. To make more valid, you may also distribute a questionnaire and conduct an interview with the potential staff.

Therefore, managers will rely on three sources of information, which are performance appraisal, supervisors/subordinates and employees. From this basis you have sufficient information to design your training modules. TNA appears to be seen as a snapshot of your future training programmes and the issue is TNA should be updated correspondingly. And TNA should also be flexible and adaptable. TNA does not always derive from problems. Training may not always the key to solve problems. For example, if there is a skills problem, therefore training will be the perfect solution. But there are many issues surrounding problems and training would be the last option. Thus, TNA will able to determine whether or not training is necessary.

Perhaps more workload would be better option rather than send some one to attend training. Training is given due to a lot of demands within the hospitality industry. Employees need more training. There are not any problems or performance discrepancies. Staffs need training because they want to learn from his/her peers. Thus, the end goal of TNA is encouraging learning. TNA comes from employees and learning is given the main reason. in the hospitality industry, training programmes come from the head-office that may not correspond with employees needs. Thus, the purpose of TNA is to modify the 'dropping' programmes that will match with staffs' desired and adjust with local culture. And this truly happens.

Taylored Training

The "core competencies" cover the skills necessary for the continued personal and organisational success in the hospitality industry, including customer service, writing, and meetings skills. To provide the training necessary to put these skills in place. The "managerial competencies" address the leadership and practical skills needed to cultivate an effective and productive managerial force, including sales, leadership and career management. Communication and team-building are the focus of the "strategic competencies" segment, and the "tactical competencies" cover sales and marketing. Taylored Training's primary resource is a panel of presenters and trainers with extensive and specialised professional experience, giving them unique understanding and insight into all facets of the hospitality industry.

Bookings through the Internet

Hotel bookings through the Internet, whether on franchise web sites or electronic distribution channels, have risen exponentially. GDS bookings increased in 2003 3. 3% while the Consumer Internet Channel bookings increased by 34. 7%. This has led many hotels and hotel companies to re-allocate sales and marketing resources to managing and manipulating their positioning on the Internet. They are quite correct in doing so—this is a trend that is not only not going away but will continue this kind of growth for at least a few years into the future. This percentage increase, unfortunately, has not been characteristic of most hotel sales departments and, as a result, the precious marketing resources available to them have, in many cases, been reduced to accommodate the expenditures on Internet channels and web presence.

As a result, many hotel sales people have become frustrated and discouraged to the point that they wonder if there is a continuing role for them as this trend continues. The traditional methods and modes of conducting hotel sales will not produce the results that will alleviate this concern. It is a simple case of "if you keep on doing what you have always done, you will continue to get what you have always gotten." In today's environment, that leads to diminishing returns as travel and meeting planners turn to the Internet more and more to evaluate rate and amenity positioning prior to ever contacting a hotel. Often, the second step is to visit the web site of a particular property, again prior to contacting the sales department. What can sales departments do to increase productivity, avoid becoming an in-house amenity. Hotels need to include the sales departments in their Internet positioning and web design so that the message and offering is consistent across the customer touch points. In addition, sales departments need to embrace the technology and use the Internet to become more productive and efficient in conducting hotel sales at every step of the sales process.

3

SERVICE QUALITY

Service organisations which offer a product that is, 'intangible dominant', increasingly seek to differentiate themselves on the basis of the software aspects such as seeking high quality and 'authentic' service interactions for the increasingly discerning customer. The key feature of inseparability is the high level of face-to-face or voice-to-voice interaction between buyer (that is, the customer) and seller resultant from the simultaneous production and consumption within the service process. This process has been variously described in hyperbolic terms as the so-called 'Moment of Truth'. Indeed, this dramaturgical view of service suggests that the organisation, via its front line staff, has to 'get it right first time' in order to ensure a flawless performance which will result in the customer returning to any given service business.

More measured and less prescriptive accounts of the service encounter are concerned to recognise a number of elements which pose a range of issues for organisations. This is particularly so on the issue of quality assurance where 'the consumer finds it difficult to isolate service quality from the quality of the service provider'. Organisations, then, may face significant problems in attempting to manage and control interaction between their front line employees and customers. These problems are given a particular focus when we recognise the notion of heterogeneity.

Heterogeneity refers to possible variations in service quality due to the labour intensity of most service production, such that 'the quality and essence of a service can vary from producer to producer, from customer to customer, and from day to day'. As a result of this possible variance in employee-customer interactions, service organisations may face difficulties in ensuring uniform quality of service between outlets, especially in branded services. One of the ways in which organisations have sought to resolve this problem is to reduce the human element in service production by the use of mechanisms such as Automatic Teller Machines in banking for example.

An alternative to this approach is to 'industrialise' services, by breaking down service operations into minute and discrete simple tasks to enable semi- and unskilled front line staff to follow a routinised, simple, standardised and often scripted approach to each service encounter, typified by fast food outlets such as McDonald's. This approach has engendered a wide literature which can broadly be seen as polarising between those who see this paradigm as one to be admired and copied or those who excoriate its dehumanising effects. Increasingly, in addressing this problem of heterogeneity, a key strategy adopted by many service organisations is extensive employee training and development. This involves organisations recognising and acting upon the idea of front line staff being crucial to organisational success and, as a result, supporting things like 'soft' HRM, internal marketing, total quality management (TQM) and empowerment.

Challenge of Evaluating Service

Service quality is more complex to evaluate than in the

case of goods. Services are more difficult to measure and standardise and consequently establishing an instrument attempting to measure quality has become a central challenge for the delivery of good service quality and service companies' success. The challenge of evaluating service quality has been motivated by recent research which increasingly demonstrates the significance of service quality as a central factor of business success. Service quality has consequently become a focus of any management and marketing strategy and high levels of service are seen as a means for organisations to achieve a competitive advantage and position themselves more effectively in the market place. Customers are also becoming more aware and critical of the alternatives on offer and rising standards of services, prompted by competitive trends, have increased customer expectations.

However, service quality may well be increasingly critical to competitive success, 'defining what exactly is "service quality" is somewhat problematic'. Generally service quality cannot be objectively measured as can technical quality for manufactured goods and it therefore remains an elusive and abstract construct. The characteristics of intangibility, heterogeneity and inseparability presented earlier also constitute a challenge for managers because they do not allow for an easy process of quality evaluation. More importantly, a customer judgement of a service depends as much on the service process as on the outcome, therefore customers' quality evaluation can be seen as depending on the production of services as well as on their consumption. The services marketing and management field has displayed different views of how this construct might be assessed.

Quality Dimensionality

Some of the researchers offer an important distinction in

their identification of process quality, which is judged by consumers during a service, from output quality, evaluated after a service has been performed. These authors also distinguished between the physical quality, relating to the physical supports of the service, corporate quality, which involves the company's image and profile, and finally interactive quality, which refers to the interactions between a consumer, the service organisation and other customers.

Another type of model proposed a division of service quality into four dimensions: technical quality, integrative quality (the ease with which different portions of the service delivery system work together), functional quality and outcome quality. Other work identified that service quality could be distinguished in two main dimensions, functional and technical quality. Hospitality has been a fertile ground for research with numerous different applications of SERVQUAL. Some of the analysis shows that the first dimension explains most of the variance observed therefore giving poor credibility to the four other dimensions and the multidimensionality of the service quality construct. Another study on hotels provided different findings from the previous application, and the reproduction of the SERVQUAL dimensions were not confirmed either.

Researchers followed step by step the SERVQUAL methodology and created a new scale, named LODGSERV, which displayed only three dimensions: tangibility, reliability and contact. To add to the confusion compared the SERVQUAL and LODGSERV scales and concluded that 'both scales fail to replicate the proposed dimensions and to provide content validity in this specific application'. Furthermore, another application of SERVQUAL to hotel and motel services identified LODGSERV but this scale simply replicated SERVQUAL to the context studied.

The SERVQUAL format commented on high expectations scores observed. Some items were also classified as dissatisfies and were defined as elements which would cause dissatisfaction by their absence but would not influence customers' satisfaction by their presence since customers assume that they would be present. Lastly, and most recently, surveyed 155 three to five star hotels in Australia using a modified version of the SERVQUAL scale. Survey aimed to test the reliability of the SERVQUAL model by establishing the number of dimensions of service quality in the hospitality industry in an attempt to determine which dimension is the best predictor of overall service quality. The amended version of SERVQUAL added eight items which were considered to specifically pertain to the hospitality industry and deleted three items. This customised version of SERVQUAL was renamed HOLSERV.

It is believed that the problems encountered in the limited generalisation of SERVQUAL might be linked to the particularities of the services upon which it was developed. Indeed, the SERVQUAL scale was built from the study of four commercial services, namely repair and maintenance, retail banking, credit card and securities brokerage. These services involve situations in which consumers buy a service for rational and functional purposes. The service delivery usually encompasses a short service encounter principally monitored by an employee and the delivery takes place in a limited environment. Indeed, most tourism and hospitality services may potentially involve complex processes, multiple encounters and a longer involvement with the service firm.

For example, the consumption of a tourist attraction involves contacts with different staff, with a multitude of tangible aspects (the attraction itself, décor, ambience, comfort, objects looked upon, rides) and the evaluation of different services provided (the attraction, restaurant, cafe, shop). Similarly, consumers using a hotel will come across a multitude of tangible aspects (the hotel, décor, layout of the rooms, atmosphere) and a variety of services (room service, cleaning, catering services, reception, bar, leisure centre).

Therefore the encounters are multiple and varied and all need to be integrated in the evaluation processes of service quality. More importantly, these different service features imply that the nature of the service delivery might follow different patterns. For example, in certain hospitality services the encounter with staff might remain relatively limited and the tangibles aspects might be quite important suggesting that the evaluation processes could be based on different criteria. This recognition of diversity is believed to be at the centre of the SERVQUAL controversy. It is recognised that the potentiality to build a generic scale is unrealistic since it would wrongly suggest that services display similar service delivery features and that customers would use similar criteria to evaluate service quality.

In fact, recognition of the limits of SERVQUAL to represent the diversity of services has already been recognised by several authors. If other services categories had been included (in the SERVQUAL scale), particularly professional services which are high in terms of opportunities for consumer intervention and adaptation, it is possible that other factor groupings would have emerged, possibly associated with one or more of the 'incorporated' dimensions: competence, credibility, security or knowledge for example. The SERVQUAL authors believed they had built their scale upon services whose 'categories were chosen to represent a broad cross-section of services that varied along key dimensions'. However, SERVQUAL was in fact built on very similar services.

Consequently, the SERVQUAL authors' conclusion that the relative importance of the dimensions identified were consistent across service settings, was considered as unrealistic. More importantly, these authors compared the relative importance of the SERVQUAL dimensions across services displaying different degrees of interaction and customisation. The relative importance of the five SERVQUAL dimensions in four new service contexts: teaching, restaurants, health care and bookstores. The results showed that the reliability dimension always remained the most important predictor of overall satisfaction for all the services investigated. However, services appeared to display different importance ratings for the dimensions according to their characteristics: in high interaction—high customisation services 'knowing the customer' was rated as the most important dimension whereas in low interaction-low customisation services, 'reliability' and 'tangibles' were the first two dimensions.

While most of the existing literature examining service quality has focused increasingly heavily on personnel contacts with customers, within certain areas of hospitality, for example hotel services, the tangible elements of the hospitality product are also extremely important. This, in part, is due to the fact that when using those services, consumers will tend to spend a longer period of time within the premises than for other services. For instance, the tangibles of a bank or a repair company can be assumed to be of lesser importance to consumers because these are not central to the service provision but also because the consumers will spend a relatively shorter period of time within those premises.

In the case of hotel services, it can be argued that since consumers will spend a longer period of time, tangibles will become a central part of the product consumption. Indeed, the notion of product consumption is key here because in a hotel, compared to a bank, as well as the longer temporal dimension customers are also consuming the tangible aspects of the room, restaurant, leisure centre and so on as an integral aspect of the core product. This is less likely to be true in a bank where the tangibles would ordinarily merely provide a meeting place between consumers and producers, they do not represent the product which is being bought and consumed by the customers.

A study on the determinants of service quality in airline services indicated that physical dimensions such as food quality or seating comfort were very important factors in service quality evaluations, again this was a service where consumers spend a relatively longer period of time in the physical space. More importantly, a recent study on hotel services clearly highlighted the specificity of that service context: 'Services differ in the proportions of tangibles they contain. It would be reasonable to suppose that the importance of tangible aspects is higher in customer experiences such as hotel services, which contain a high proportion of clearly differentiated tangible components'.

Whilst hotels can be both labour and capital intensive it is the former which has often generated the greatest interest and initiatives: The modern hotel industry has tended to promote its obsession with customer service delivery standards while ignoring the need for the hotel product to meet the expectations of the customer. Put another way 'soft' human and interactional processes are promoted as the principle means of ensuring customer satisfaction to the extent that attention to the 'hard' elements of the hospitality product is diminished. Customer expectations have evolved and that evidence points to an increasing interest in the quality of the product rather than the service.

Scepticism of the need for organisations to consider the softer aspects of the service encounter, much of the work that has emerged in relation to more prescriptive accounts of service quality have tended to point to the human dimension. Thus, although the tangibles are perceived as being important, the human dimension through the employee service is also particularly relevant.

In sum, customer perceptions of quality will vary from service to service and will, at various times, encompass different aspects. Indeed, in many respects notions of service quality may be as much about consistent delivery to the specified offer, whether high or low specification.

As a corollary, this review of the dimensionality of service quality clearly reinforces the notion that the relative importance of quality dimensions will change between a fast food restaurant and Michelin starred restaurant or a basic budget hotel and a deluxe hotel. Equally this also points to the obvious point that differing HRM approaches are likely to be appropriate to differing service settings and it is this issue which is now considered by firstly reflecting upon the relationship generally between competitive strategy and HRM before moving on to the service sector specifically.

Competitive Marketing Strategies and HRM

One of the earliest and most influential attempts to develop a model which theorised the relationship between competitive strategy and HRM was that offered by Schuler and Jackson. Building on the earlier seminal work undertaken by Porter on competitive strategy, and particularly routes to gaining competitive advantage, Schuler and Jackson developed a series of typologies of 'needed role behaviours' that enabled the link between competitive strategy and HRM practices to be made.

The type of needed role behaviours within Schuler and Jackson's model was contingent on the overall strategies that an organisation could adopt to seek competitive advantage and the concomitant HRM approached adopted to sustain this. First, there is an innovation strategy, where organisations seek to develop products or services which are different from competitors, such that the focus here is on companies offering something new and different.

Organisations adopting this approach seek to develop an environment where innovation is allowed to flourish. Resultantly, the employee needed role behaviour in such a scenario is characterised by things like a willingness to tolerate ambiguity and unpredictability, the need to be creative and risk taking. Given these characteristics the type of HRM strategy flowing from this approach is based on having a large number of highly skilled individuals who are likely to enjoy high levels of autonomy.

Second, is the quality enhancement strategy wherein firms seek to gain competitive advantage by enhancing the product and/or service quality. The approach once again points to certain HRM practices to support a total quality approach. These practices include the encouragement of feedback systems, teamwork, decision making and responsibility being an integral part of an employees job description and flexible job classifications.

The intent of these practices is to create needed employee behaviour such as co-operative, interdependent behaviour, and commitment to the goals of the organisation. Lastly, the cost reduction strategy sees firms attempting to gain competitive advantage by aiming to be the lowest cost producer within a particular market segment. The characteristics of firms seeking to pursue this strategy are tight controls, minimisation of overheads and pursuit of economies of scale, in the pursuit of increased productivity.

In following such a strategy organisations may use higher number of part timers, seek to simplify and measure work via narrowly defined jobs that encourage specialisation and efficiency, and offer short-term results oriented appraisal. Needed employee behaviours include, repetitive and predictable behaviour, low risk taking activity and a high degree of comfort with stability.

As Schuler and Jackson freely admit the description of these three competitive strategies as pure types often does not reflect the reality of, for example, organisations pursuing two or more competitive strategies simultaneously. Nevertheless, this work remains useful for its clear delineation of differing approaches to HRM and the concomitant support for a 'best fit' approach to HRM. Although not necessarily explicitly providing the basis for much of the work which has emerged on these questions in the more specific context of the services marketing and management literature, the influence of Schuler and Jackson can clearly be seen.

Clearly Bowen et al. are arguing for the importance of HRM practices 'fitting' the organisations own strategically defined market segment. This support for the need to generate congruence between the three crucial functional areas of marketing, operations and HRM is commonplace in much of the service marketing and management literature. Indeed, in an earlier work Schneider and Bowen warned organisations not to fall into what they term the 'human resources trap', wherein service firms place excess reliance on their employees as a means to customer satisfaction. Even, then, within the more prescriptive work on service management generally there is a clear recognition of the need for a measured reading of the relationship between product market strategies and HRM. Again, though not explicitly mentioning the work of Schuler and Jackson, Lashley and Taylor's work evidences much the same thinking in their description of four basic archetypes within which hospitality organisations can be potentially located.

Having firstly offered the caveat as to the extent to which the strategy making process remains rational and clearly developed by managers, Lashley and Taylor go on to advocate a 'hierarchy of effects' that should flow from the strategic level down and through functional and tactical levels. They further note, 'In simple terms having formulated its basic mission statement, the service organisation would decide upon both its marketing and competitive strategy.' Lashley and Taylor developed their model by utilising matrices provided by Schmenner and Heskett et al. to identify different processes in service operations management. These processes are the service factory, the service shop, mass service and professional services.

These characterisations are based on the degree of customisation and labour intensity involved in the service offer, in terms of the degree of customer contact required between employees and customers. The service factory is relatively low labour intensity and low customisation, i.e. high standardisation. The service factory is most obviously exemplified by fast food operators, especially McDonald's. The service shop involves more customisation, but relatively low labour intensity. The defining difference to the service factory lies in the degree of standardisation within the process. Lashley and Taylor draw upon the example of TGI Fridays to argue that although there are high levels of standardisation in the tangible aspects of the organisation, such as the menus, layouts, décor and staff uniform, there is also some scope to customise the customers' eating and drinking experience.

This customisation is by virtue of their more extensive menu, and more importantly, greater spontaneity and authenticity in the intangible aspects of the service provided by front-line staff. The next classification is mass service where service processes involve a relatively high degree of labour intensity, though a limited amount of customisation. Lashley and Taylor assert that the Marriott hotel brand typifies a mass service organisation. The rationale for such an assertion lies in the fact that their four star offering is similar to others in relation to the hardware of the tangibles reflecting the highly competitive nature of the mid to upper segment of the hotel market.

4

Bar Management

Bar is a business that sells alcoholic beverages for immediate on-premise consumption. Some bars serve food or may be parts of restaurants. Bars that are part of hotels are sometimes called *long bars*. Alternatively, "bar" can refer to the specialized counter on which the drinks are served, and it is from this term that the establishment itself as a whole gets its name. The "back bar" is a (sometimes ornate) set of shelves of glasses and bottles behind that counter. Frequently when food is served elsewhere in the establishment, it may also be ordered and consumed at the bar.

From a business standpoint, however, a bar can provide an excellent return on investment. Before you get started on the actual nuts and bolts of creating your dream bar, you have to decide what kind of establishment you'd like to own. Let's take a trip through the various kinds of bars—from neighbourhood bar to large-scale nightclub—and see which one is right for you.

Neighbourhood Bar

Conceptually, the neighbourhood bar is still an American version of the English pub. You'll find them everywhere in the United States. If you own this kind of place, you can expect to know a great deal of your regular customers. As on the TV show "Cheers," you may find yourself taking phone messages for customers or cashing their paychecks. It's because of the friendly "home away from home" atmosphere that neighbourhood bars are successful. Some of these pubs open as early as 6 a.m., and they sometimes close earlier than other bars—depending on the clientele. This type of bar is perfect for small-scale entertainment options, such as darts, pool tables, video games and jukeboxes. Across the country, this is probably the most popular type of bar you'll find.

But there are a lot of neighbourhoods out there, so you might find that there is room for one more in your area. According to the experts the start-up cost for this kind of bar can range anywhere from $20,000 to $200,000, depending on the size and concept. The amount of revenue these businesses produce varies greatly depending on geographical location—big city or small town—and the size of the bar.

Sports Bar

Depending on the establishment's capacity, sports bars can be a specific version of the neighbourhood tavern, or they can take on a life as big as a nightclub. You may have the latter in mind, but your market research may point to the former. It's important to do your homework! Generally, sports bars offer some kind of menu options, such as sandwiches, burgers, pizza and appetizers. Since the main attraction is sporting events, sports bars have televisions in view of every seat, sometimes all tuned to different channels. Audio and video technology comes into play, with some owners spending a large percentage of their revenue on keeping up with the latest in technology—from satellites to big-screen TVs. The startup costs and revenue potential reflect basically the same numbers as a neighbourhood bar.

Beer Bar

Studies have shown that although consumers are drinking less alcohol, their tastes are becoming more discriminating. As a result, microbrews are becoming more and more popular. In a brewpub, you can brew your own beer right on the premises. In a beer bar, you can offer a large selection of different types of beer, including microbrews produced elsewhere. It's often easier to get a liquor license for a brewpub or beer bar than a full-scale liquor license since you don't need a fully stocked liquor bar.

Most brewpubs only sell their own beer options on tap (draft beer), with a few selections of bottled beer options, too. Since you're creating your own product in a brewpub, you also have the ability to control what you make and sell—from quality to quantity. The startup costs of a brewpub can be quite high—from $100,000 to $1 million—because of the brewing equipment you need to have. If you produce a popular beer, you have the opportunity to grow into a very successful operation to make two or three times your startup costs.

Beer bars tend to have lower startup costs, which can often mean obtaining a less expensive, fixed-price license from your state government. Beer bar startup costs range from about $20,000 to $100,000, depending on size and location. The revenue potential depends on the geographical location and drinking trends in the community.

Wine and Champagne Bar

This kind of bar often gives guests the opportunity to taste a variety of different kinds of wines and the ability to learn more about their qualities. Wine and champagne bars tend to stay small and intimate in size and are located in more sophisticated neighbourhoods.

Again, because you only need a beer and wine license to open this type of bar, your licensing fees drop considerably. Depending on the type of product you serve and the extent of your decor, you can expect to find the cost and revenues close to the amounts for a beer bar.

Nightclub

Like the neighbourhood bar, nightclubs can take on a number of different personalities. You can open a small "cocktail lounge" with a jukebox or a tinkling piano in the corner. A medium-sized nightclub might look like a neighbourhood bar during the lunchtime hours, then spring to life with a popular band at night. Or if you have a big enough budget, your nightclub might be a large dance club where the most fashionable people and hippest celebrities hang out every weekend. Whichever path you take, you must be prepared to spend a great deal of time and money on promotion to create your "buzz." Nightclubs can make plenty of money if they're managed properly.

As a bar owner, you need to embark on the same kind of relentless detective work to profile your customers before you start investing large sums of money in your business. The majority of the research material you need is probably already available to you. You simply have to compile it. You can go about developing your customer profile in several different ways, then compare the results to determine your direction.

— *General demographics*: Your bar's concept may go in a totally different direction if you're in a college town with a high percentage of young, single students than if you're in a quiet, conservative suburb populated with families.

— *Alcohol trends*: National and regional alcohol suppliers keep records of how their product fits into the market.

Your potential suppliers can provide valuable information about your customers and what they like to drink. Generally, they are glad to help. If you do your research and have a successful bar, your suppliers will profit, too.

— *Other important statistics*: Visit your local public library or university library. Many libraries have business departments that have a wealth of information about demographics, income levels and spending trends.

— *Lifestyle trends*: Call the lifestyle and entertainment editors at your local newspaper and regional magazines, as well as the advertising and marketing departments of local radio stations. They can give you information about your competitors and tell you more about the establishments that have been successful in the area.

— *Your customers and the competition:* You can discover a ton of information about your customers using internet resources. Besides general demographics, you can surf the web for information about other bars in the area. Pop into chat areas and newsgroups to find out where the action is and which bars are the hot spots.

Research and Development

Once you've compiled all your research, you can devise a concrete profile of your clientele. For example, you may decide your target customers are professionals between the ages of 30 and 50 who have incomes of more than $35,000 and like jazz music. Whatever you set as your target market will affect all the decisions you make from here on, so make sure you get it right! Once you have your profile, you can develop your menu and bar inventory based on what customers like. Look for trade magazines and industry associations that provide data on food and beverage spending patterns.

Keep in mind that you may have more than one profile to work with. You may have a conservative professional clientele during the daytime and a rowdy college crowd at night. If you use your research wisely, you can develop a bar that caters to both profiles for even more business. The bar/tavern industry can be a pricey undertaking. Because of the high failure rate, you may come across desperate bar owners willing to take a low purchase price just to get out of the business. You'll also find that startup costs for bars vary depending on size, location and target market.

Your bar's size, location, type and concept will make your startup cost as individual as your business. Again, you could buy an existing bar that would nullify all the numbers on our low-end chart, or start a large-scale nightclub that's off the map from our high-end numbers. You'll have to do some research to find out what your bar will cost based on your concept, size and location.. The groundwork you lay to operate your bar includes the systems you use to track liquor and food. How much does the customer owe the server/bartender, and in turn, how much do they owe you? Also, what liquor and food do you sell the most? The systems you choose depend on the type and size of bar you have.

In most bars, only the bartenders and servers handle money. Cashiers or takeout staff may also have cash-handling responsibilities. Factors to consider when choosing an accounting system include the level of sales you expect, both from alcohol and food, and the efficiency needed for your staff to operate at its full potential. Also, look for holes that your accounting system might leave open for theft at all levels, not just servers and bartenders. No one thinks they are hiring a thief.

Many people who might steal if the opportunity arose do not consider themselves thieves, either, so they don't come off as such. If you use the cash-and-carry system, where the drink is ordered by the server verbally and then paid for before the bartender or server rings it up, you might find many "forgot to ring it up" drinks, as well as a few given away for free. It is the nature of the system. If your inventory controls are so tight that you will notice when too much has been used, or if your manager, who shares in the profits anyway, is your bartender, then you can use this system without much fear.

Choice of Location

Your choice of location will depend on how you want your bar to look, what you want your bar to contribute to the community, and the kind of clientele you want to patronise it. Then you need to decide whether you want to buy the location or sign a lease. Again, that depends on your budget. Finally, you need to figure out how to fuse your concept with both your name and your location to your best advantage. People who know this industry well have polar opinions on the concept of location. Some owners and experts put enormous importance on the bar's location while others refuted its significance altogether.

It all depends on what you want your bar to be and what your strengths are as an owner. If you want your bar to get impulsive neighbourhood traffic in a particular area, then you should be closest, and most obvious, to them. If you'd rather spend the time and money, saved by more affordable real estate, to develop your establishment's concept and create your own buzz and destination, your actual location won't matter so much. You should consider factors such as safety, parking, accessibility to customers—even the history of the site—when choosing a location.

Naming

When it comes to naming a bar, experts generally fall into

two major schools of thought. The first says your bar is your dream—your hard work—so you should name it anything you want. The second approach to naming says your moniker is the first and greatest form of advertising for your drinking establishment. Now that you have your entertainment in place and ready to go, it's time to start planning how you're going to get people into your bar to enjoy it. Just like any other aspect of operating your bar, marketing is an ongoing process.

Many bar owners think marketing is the most fun and exciting aspect of running a bar. There are still ways to get some advertising and marketing out there without spending a ton of money. But anytime you reach into your own pocket to buy advertising for a bar, it's not good. Your employees love working there. They are talking and saying great things about the place, and that is passed on to your customers. The customers love being there, and they tell other customers. If you can get to that point, it's just priceless." You can create special promotions for your bar, launch a direct-mail campaign with a newsletter for regular customers, develop a web site, and any other creative marketing techniques you can dream up.

Promotion

Most bars are busy on Friday and Saturday nights, with Thursdays coming in third place. You might decide you need to pump up business on Monday or Tuesday, so pick one day and keep it going until you have established enough regular business to move the promotions to a different day. Promoting your bar can be fun and creative. During a promotion and after it's over, ask your customers and your employees for feedback and critiques. Of course, your sales will give you a lot of the information you're looking for, too.

Gross Profit

Beverage costs must be controlled if an operation is to reach maximum potential of gross profit from beverage sales. Every reduction in beverage cost percentage renders a higher gross profit. Beverage costs that are above industry averages can negatively impact your profitability. A profitable restaurant typically generates a 22% to 28% beverage cost. Because of the impact beverage costs can make on an operation, it is important to know where beverage cost falls in relation to total sales on a daily or weekly basis. Beyond the bottom line, beverage costs also reflect an operation's control systems, management skill level, and value provided to the customers. Many restaurant managers do not calculate beverage cost correctly, or if they do, they do not fully understand the process. If calculated correctly, the ratio can be compared to industry averages and previous performance.

Alcoholic beverages are included in beverage cost calculations. Soft drinks, juices, coffees, and other non-alcoholic beverage sales are included in food cost calculations. With an accurate beverage cost, steps can be taken to improve the operation and ultimately improve the bottom line. The industry standard is based on the Uniform System of Accounts for Restaurants. This system clearly identifies what items are included in each part of the beverage cost formula and is briefly outlined below.

Beverage Cost = Cost of Beverage Sales / Total Beverage Sales

The beverage sales and costs should be generated during a set accounting time period of at least two weeks or more typically, every 28 days, or monthly. Soft drinks, juices, coffee, and other non-alcoholic beverage sales are included in *food* cost calculations, not beverage cost calculations.

Sales of Beverage

This is the relatively easy part—total the customer checks or reports from point-of-sale registers—making sure to only include sales generated from beverage sources (sources other than beverage should be allocated to a "food" or "other income" account). The costs associated with beverage sales are comprised of *purchases* and *inventory level adjustments*. In our experience, this part of the calculation is often computed incorrectly. Equally important, and often not included in determining cost of beverage sales, is the inventory adjustment.

Many restaurants consider only purchases in determining beverage cost. This does not create an accurate beverage cost percentage—depending on the day purchases are made and what the cut-off date is for including sales in the beverage cost calculation, your beverage cost could appear higher or lower than it actually is. Additionally, this discrepancy makes it difficult to compare and track beverage costs. For example, suppose you receive (purchase) all your spirits and wine products on Thursday to prepare for the weekend. The time period for determining beverage cost ends on Friday (the next day). In calculating your beverage cost, it appears much higher than last month. While the increase may be due to theft or another operational issue, most likely it is due to calculating your beverage cost inconsistently and incorrectly. Your purchases reflect a large Thursday delivery, however, you do not log the sales from the weekend to offset these purchases, making your beverage cost appear out of line. Additionally, you have not factored in the inventory adjustment.

To properly determine beverage cost, a physical inventory of the main bar, service bar and storeroom areas must be conducted at the end of each period. Once you have your ending period inventory level, look at the *change* from your beginning (start of time period) inventories (bars and storerooms). The key to accurate cost determination is understanding the role inventory levels play. Considering this change and its effect on cost of beverage sales, apply the difference to the total purchases for the time period, giving you the total cost of beverage sales.

Cost of Beverage Sales =Purchases+/- Inventory Adjustment

Successful restaurants generate beverage costs in the mid 20% range. However, different types of operations typically run higher or lower percentages—fine dining may run up to 35% (sales of bottles of wine are usually less profitable other alcoholic beverages) whereas brewpub restaurants may run about 15%. Comparing your cost percentage to restaurants with similar menus and service levels provides a more accurate perspective.

5

DINING SERVICES

Restaurants range from unpretentious lunching or dining places catering to people working nearby, with simple food served in simple settings at low prices, to expensive establishments serving refined food and wines in a formal setting. In the former case, customers usually wear casual clothing. In the latter case, depending on culture and local traditions, customers might wear semi-casual, semi-formal, or even in rare cases formal wear. Standardly customers sit at tables, their orders are taken by a waiter, who brings the food when it is ready, and the customers pay the bill before leaving.

In finer restaurants there will be a host or hostess or even a maître d'hôtel to welcome customers and to seat them. Other staff waiting on customers include busboys and sommeliers. Depending on local custom, a tip of varying proportions of the bill (often 10–20%) may be added, which (usually) goes to the staff rather than the restaurant. This gratuity might be added directly to the bill or it may be given voluntarily. Restaurants often specialise in certain types of food or present a certain unifying, and often entertaining, theme.

For example, there are seafood restaurants, vegetarian restaurants or ethnic restaurants. Generally speaking, restaurants selling "local" food are simply called restaurants, while restaurants selling food of foreign origin are called accordingly, for example, a *Chinese restaurant* and a *French restaurant*. Depending on local customs and the establishment, restaurants may or may not serve alcoholic beverages. Restaurants are often prohibited from selling alcohol without a meal by alcohol sale laws; such sale is considered to be activity for bars, which are meant to have more severe restrictions. Some restaurants are licensed to serve alcohol ("fully licensed"), and/or permit customers to "bring your own" alcohol.

The host is a key player in a restaurant's moment of truth. Many times, the first employee of the restaurant who comes in contact with the guests is the host. The host may also be responsible for training and managing the service employees in the dining room. The service staff have many moments of truth with the guests. Karl Albrecht states that there are seven deadly sins concerning service. Being aware of them and of how to prevent them is the obligation of both the host and the service staff. The seven deadly sins of service are: apathy, the brush-off, coldness, condescension, robotism, rule book excuses, and the runaround.

Apathy can be described as a lack of emotion or interest. An example of an apathetic host is found in the following example: The guest enters the restaurant and sees the host standing at the host's desk (the podium). The host does not acknowledge the guest's presence. Instead, the host appears to be interested in reading something that is much more important than greeting the guests. To avoid the sin of apathy, greet guests immediately when they enter the restaurant. Studies have shown that the impression made in the first thirty seconds of contact between the guest and the restaurant determines the feeling of the guest about the total dining experience.

This is the first moment of truth for the restaurant. The host can create a positive one by greeting the guest within thirty seconds of arrival.

Brush-off is a slang term that means rebuff, according to The Random House Dictionary.' Relating it to the host's job, an example of brushing off the guest occurs in the following cases: The guest approaches the host and asks (usually in a timid manner), "When will my table be ready? You told me it would be ready now and it isn't." The host replies, "In a few minutes," and walks away from the guest without any explanation or comment. The second moment of truth has been negative for the restaurant. To prevent committing the second sin, the host should strive to give the guest undivided attention. To avoid brushing off the guest, the host could apologise to the guest and assure the guest that the party will be seated as soon as possible. The host will then seat that party when the next table is available. If the problem persists and a table is not ready, it becomes the responsibility of the host to tell the guest about the status of the seating. Eye contact should be made with the guests, so that they do not get the impression that the host is trying to brush them off.

Have you even been to a restaurant where the food was excellent and the prices reasonable, but you still felt something was missing? That something was a problem that you could not identify. Most of the time, it was that the restaurant left you with a cold feeling toward it. The host who responds to the guest's question with one-phrase or one-word answers is guilty of committing the sin of coldness. For example, a guest might ask the host, "How long has the restaurant been in business?" The host answers, "Two years." The next question is also answered with a brisk reply. This is the one opportunity for the host to make the guest the restaurant's ally; instead, the host has turned off the guest. Answers are best if they are complete and friendly. This will benefit the restaurant in two ways. First, the guest will have questions answered, and second, it will create a warm feeling toward the restaurant by the guest.

Condescension can be described as an air of superiority that an individual shows toward another person. A host who is guilty of the sin of condescension would give the guest the impression that he or she does not belong in the restaurant. Unfortunately, condescension is, frequently directed at high school students. This most often occurs when they have a prom, and go to the dinner before the dance. The host's attitude conveys the impression to the staff that the high school students are not very good customers. Notice the word customers is used, not guests, That is an example of a condescending attitude.

To correct this problem, the host should lead by setting an example, and should treat all the individuals who enter the restaurant as guests. All guests receiving positive treatment by all employees will increase repeat business for the establishment. The host or the staff should not be allowed to feel that they are better than any of the guests. By treating the high school student as guests, and by realising that this is an important night for them, the host can make them feel important. Therefore, the host should greet them warmly and treat them like the valued, respectable guests they are.

Robots do not belong in the dining room of a restaurant. A robot can do many repetitive, boring tasks well. However, the job of the host is not repetitive or boring. An example of robotism is when the host seats guests. The host picks up the menus; says, "Follow me"; and sprints to the table. The host then places the menus at the place settings and says, "Have a good meal." The next group of people are treated to the same robotic antics. This method of dealing with guests is eventually transferred to the actions of the service staff. It becomes especially obvious when the service person is going through the "Hi, my name is..." canned speech. To alleviate the sin of robotism, the host should act natural, and should encourage the staff to act natural also. The host's movements should be energetic, and his or her speech should be cordial toward the guests. A robot would be great to do the dishes, but not to manage the dining room.

Rules are a necessary part of any business. However, when a host manages only by rules, and does not use common sense, the restaurant will suffer. A couple decided to try a new restaurant that had windows overlooking beautiful view. The tables directly in front of the windows were all booths for four people. When the hostess seated them at a deuce away from the windows, they asked for a window seat. The hostess said "I'm sorry but I have to save those seats for parties of four." They tried to buy the table by giving her a five-dollar bill. She still said that she could not give them the table. The time was 5 P.m., just when the restaurant opened and there were no other guests demanding to be seated. They could not understand why they could not have the table they desired. During their meal, they watched the table to see how many people she sat at the booths. When they left an hour and a half later, there still were no guests seated at the table they wanted. Of course, they never returned to the restaurant-and apparently not too many others did either, because the restaurant went out of business. This was another example of a host failing at the moment of truth. The host must not fall victim of the sin of rule book excuses, and may bend the rules when it benefits the guests.

The final sin of service has been experienced by everyone at one time or another in life-the runaround. An example of this as it relates to the host often occurs when the guest is waiting for a table at a no-reservation restaurant. When the guest approaches the host and asks how long it will be before the party is seated, the host replies, "Just a short time." The guest waits for a table to be vacant, and after twenty minutes returns to the host and asks the same question. Again the host says it will be just a short while. When the guest demands a specific time, the host pretends to check the dining room and gets sidetracked. The definition of the runaround is to give vague answers or to refuse to answer the question by ignoring or changing the meaning of the question. The way to avoid the runaround is for the host to give definite answers.

A definite time will satisfy the guest's question of "How long will it be before the table is ready?" An appropriate answer would be fifteen to twenty minutes, not "In a short while." Knowing and training the staff to recognise and avoid the seven deadly sins of service is important for the host. The restaurant business is filled with many moments of truth. The restaurant cannot afford to have sins committed at any moment of truth. The first moment of truth comes when the host greets guests into the restaurant. The last moment occurs when the guest leaves the establishment. Throughout their meal, they will experience a series of moments of truth. All of these moments of truth add up to the total service in the restaurant. If the staff fail in one of these moments of truths, then service will suffer.

Greeting the Guests

The greeting should be warm and cordial, just as it would be in the host's home. The first thirty seconds are critical for the guest. In those few seconds, the guest forms an opinion about the restaurant: it wants or does not want the guest's business. This is all determined from the greeting offered by the host. The size and volume of the restaurant determine the number of hosts on duty and their responsibilities. Smaller restaurants usually have one host who has to perform all the jobs. At larger establishments there may be as many as four hosts. One remains at the podium to greet guests, take names, and assign tables. Another finds the guests in the waiting area or at the bar. The other two show the guests to their tables, each being responsible for one half of the dining room. Other establishments use three hosts. One remains at the podium to greet guests, take names, and assign tables.

Another gets the guests when their table is ready. The third seats people and does table checks. Regardless of the size of the establishment or the number of hosts employed, one host is always responsible for greeting the guests. This individual is always in a position to see when a guest enters the restaurant. Once the guest enters the restaurant, it becomes the host's responsibility to greet the guests immediately. If the host recognises the guests, he or she will greet them by addressing them by name. If the guests are new to the restaurant, the greeting is cordial. When at the podium receiving guests, the host should not be leaning over the desk, chewing gum, smoking, or drinking. Instead, the guests receive the undivided attention of the host.

Assigning Tables

As with everything else in the restaurant business, there is a correct way to assign tables. There are also those hosts who take shortcuts and create problems for the guests, service staff, and the restaurant. Assigning tables correctly is another step to ensure that the restaurant obtains maximum income and the guests receive excellent service. A good tactic used by many restaurants is to seat the guests who arrive when the restaurant opens at a table by the window. Studies have shown that people would rather dine in a busy restaurant than one that is not busy. If the host seats guests near a window, people walking or driving by will see the guests enjoying a meal, and it will create an impression in their minds that the restaurant is a good place to dine. Rotation of the seating of the guests among the different stations is also advised. The wrong way to seat guests is for the host to seat the first twenty guests at one station. Instead, the first party is seated at station one, the second at station two, and so on.

Rotating the seating in this manner allows the service person to give the guests excellent service. If the service person's station were filled up all at once, the service person would have difficulty giving the guests good service because he or she would be overwhelmed with too many guests to serve at once. The rotation of assigning tables is also considered when stations are made and reservations are being blocked. Occasionally a guest will request a special table or a different table from the one the host assigns. If the host can honour the request, it is good policy to do it. If there is a legitimate reason not to honour the request, it should be explained to the guest.

For example, many times guests will request a 4-top for their party of two. If there is not too much business forecasted for the day, the host can give them the table they desire. If the host expects a heavy demand of business or has a reservation for the table they desire, the guests should be told the reason why they cannot have the table. Of course, if they are regular guests, the host should try to accommodate them and provide them the table. Always seat parties of two at 4-tops if those tables are not in demand. When a large group of people request a table together, the host should inquire whether they are on a time schedule (sometimes guests are attending a conference and have only a limited time to eat). If they are, it would be wise for the host to explain that it would be faster service if the party broke up into groups of four.

Host Needs

In addition to the ability to think quickly, the host needs a few forms that will assist in doing the job correctly and efficiently. The forms needed are: a diagram of the tables in the restaurant, the reservation list, the turnsheet, a table check form, and a waitlist. At the host's desk, there should be a diagram of the floor plan of the restaurant. Many restaurants place this diagram under a glass top. The hosts are given a grease pencil so they can write on the glass to indicate the vacant or occupied status of the table. Using the grease pencil and glass top makes it easier for the host to keep track of the status of the tables. It is also easier to erase and neater than trying to keep track on individual paper diagrams.

Along with the diagram of the restaurant, the host should also have an alphabetised list of the names of the guests who have reserved a table. Included on the list should be the names of the guests, the number of guests, and the table number they have been assigned. The list should be set up in chronological order. This will allow the host to check off the names as the guests come in to the restaurant, and will make for a smoother operation. The listing would continue throughout the entire day. By setting this up in an organised fashion, the host can spend time attending to the guests' needs. If the host did not write this seating out in advance, he or she would have to spend an enormous amount of time and effort correctly seating the guests with reservations.

The next form needed to seat guests effectively is called a turnsheet. The turnsheet shows that have five service staff. After each person's name there is a series of numbers. The top number of the fraction represents the number of guests in the party. Most hosts use the turnsheet to seat the guests equitably among the service staff. However, when the restaurant becomes busy, often the host has no choice but to seat the guests at the next available table. However, in order to avoid a controversy with the service staff, it is advisable for the host to keep track of the guests served by using the turnsheet. Restaurants that do not take reservations, or only reserve a small percentage of tables, need a method to seat the guests. When there are tables available, there are no problems; guests are seated at an available table.

Problems arise when all tables are occupied. No guest wants to be treated in the following manner. In this no-reservations policy restaurant, when guests approached the host and asked for a table, the host would seat them. However, if the dining room was full, the host would tell the guest to go to the bar and check back in a few moments. The guest would say, "Aren't you going to put my name down?" The host would reply, "No." The guest wanted to know how he would know when his table would be ready. `Just come back, and if there is a table you get it," said the host. The guest suggested that a better method would be to take his name down. The host replied, "What do you think I am, a secretary?" The host is no longer employed at this establishment.

Checking of Table

The table check is a tool that allows the host to know the point of the meal that each table has reached. This form is continuously updated throughout the meal. For instance, some restaurants will have it done every twenty minutes. The table check is completed by one of the hosts whose job it is to walk around the dining room and observe each table's progress. Some restaurants do table checks every twenty minutes, while other hosts do table checks informally. The host remains at the desk greeting guests, while another employee roams throughout the dining room, communicating the -availability of the tables directly to the host via a headset microphone. Once the host knows how long the wait will be, the proper method of informing the guest of the wait for the table can be used.

Waiting Time

When a guest arrives at a restaurant that does not take reservations and there is a long waiting time, the host has an obligation to tell the guests approximately how long they will have to wait for a table. Most guests do not mind waiting; however, some guests will object. The host should never state to a guest that it will just be a few minutes for a table. Instead, the host should give the guest an approximate time. This time has to be one that the host can honour. For example, if the host knows that a table will be vacant in fifteen minutes, the guest should be told that there is a wait of fifteen to twenty minutes. If the guest is seated before the fifteen minutes, that will be great for the guest. If the wait is more than twenty minutes, the restaurant has failed in this moment of truth. When the host informs the guest of the length of the wait, the responsibility of staying or leaving rests upon the guest.

Many restaurants have a friendly working relationship with their competitors. The host will phone the competitors and find out how long a wait there is at the competitor's restaurant, if any. The host can use this information in a variety of ways to assist the guests. First, if there is a long wait at the competitor's restaurant, this knowledge relayed to the guests may keep them at the host's restaurant. This is especially true after the guests have to factor in driving time to the competitor's restaurant. However, if the competitor has space available or a much shorter waiting list, this can be relayed to the guests. The host should keep the guests informed whenever possible about problems that arise that may keep the table from being available when promised.

If guests cannot be seated when promised, management policy may allow the host to give the guests some complimentary item to let them know that their business is appreciated. One restaurant takes this a step further. Any guests who are told the waiting time and decide that it is too long for them to stay, receive a card that can be redeemed for a complimentary drink on their next visit to the restaurant.

Use of Waitlist

The waitlist is used when all the tables are occupied in the restaurant and guests are waiting for a table. The waitlist is set up with the names of the guests who are waiting for a table. The next column is for guests who want a table for four or more guests. The number in parenthesis, 51, represents the table that the host plans to use for that party. Est. wait time refers to the amount of time the host has estimated that the guest will have to wait for a table. Time in refers to when the guest entered the restaurant. Time seated is when the guest has been seated at the table. The next column is for groups of two. Finally, the table number where the guest was actually seated is recorded.

Methods of Informing Guests

Different establishments have different methods for informing their guests when their tables are ready. Many have loudspeakers that announce their names. A more professional method is to have a system that instructs the bartenders and cocktail servers to ask the guests if they are having dinner. If the guests say they are, they ask them for their card. When their table is ready, the host calls the bar and informs the bartender that there is a table available for the Smith party of two.

Another method is for the host to walk through the waiting area and announce the names of the guests that he or she is seeking. At a twentieth-year high school reunion, a classmate boasted that he had never waited very long for a table at places that had a no-reservation policy. He and his date would go to restaurants that took the names of walk-in guests waiting for a table. Sometimes, they would go to the bar and have a drink; other times they would obtain their table immediately. This is how he did it: As soon as he heard the host calling the name and number of guests in the party, he would go to the host and claim the table.

Most of the time he was seated because the restaurant did not give out any cards to the guests. Another method uses technology. Guests waiting for a table are given pagers and allowed to roam the vicinity. When their table is ready, they are beeped by the host. Of course, a few pagers may be lost by forgetful patrons. The host must keep an accurate waitlist to avoid problems in seating guests, and to aid in planning future business. All restaurants have their own codes to assist them with the waitlist. At one restaurant, when a guest requests a table for six, the host places a big black mark around the guest's name. This is to signify that they have a large party waiting.

As the number of tables that will accommodate six people are limited, the host does not want to make the guest's party wait longer than they are told. In addition, once the host sends for a party, he or she underlines the name with the black pen. When the person has been located, the host puts a double mark under the name. If a person is not found, he or she puts down the time the guest was called, gives them fifteen minutes to appear, and if they are not there in that time, puts in large letters NS (for No-Show) through their name.

The information gained from the waitlist can be valuable for the host. The host can see how many guests had to wait for a table, the time the first guest had to wait, the average waiting time, the longest waiting time, and other factors that will help the host staff and plan for the business. Once the host reaches the table, it is proper to pull out chairs for the guests (women first) and assist them with seating. If the table is against the wall, it has become traditional to offer the seat that faces into the dining room to the female, while the male is seated facing the wall. The napkins are removed from the table by the host, opened, and handed to the guests. Menus should be distributed next, both food and wine, if appropriate.

Many hosts bring the guest to the table, drop off the menus, and are never seen again. After the guests have been seated and handed menus, the host should inform the guests of any chef's creations (and their prices) that are not listed on the written menu. The restaurant should not have more than three chef's specials, because the guests may become confused. Many restaurants use an alternative method. The host gives a list of daily specials to the guests along with the regular menus. The host points out the list, which includes prices, to the guests as they are seated. It is strongly suggested that the host use the guests' names as much as possible when they are known.

Once the guests have been told the additions to the menu, the host may also ask them if they would like to order a beverage. This is a key moment of truth in the restaurant business. By having the host take the drink order, the guest will have been served immediately. The restaurant is saying to the guest that we value your business and do not want you to wait for anything. In addition, there is the possibility of selling more drinks, whether they are alcoholic or nonalcoholic. This serving or taking of a drink order should be done with every meal period. At breakfast, the host would offer coffee to the guest immediately. The last thing the host should do as he leaves the table is to tell the guests the name of the service person.

Communicate with Guests

Working the floor is a phrase used in the restaurant business to mean that the host is circulating around the dining room talking to guests and assisting service staff. When the guest has been seated by the host, the host should not go back and stand at the podium waiting for the next guest to come into the restaurant. Instead, the host has to walk around the dining room and make certain that the guests are being served properly.

One of the key factors in working the floor is to communicate with the guests. If the host notices that the guests are sitting at the table with their menus for a long period of time, he should approach the table and ask, "Has Jan been here to take your order yet?" Working the floor also involves "getting your hands dirty." This means that the host (and dining room manager, if they are not the same . person) may bus tables, serve food, serve drinks, and reset tables if a service person needs assistance.

The host should be not just a pretty face but a vital working member of the staff. The final responsibility of the host is to make sure that the guests are completely satisfied with their dining experience. As the guests complete their meals, the host inquires about their dining experience and shows appreciation to the guests for patronising the restaurant. This appreciation can be shown in the form of a "Thank you," buying the guest a free dessert or after-dinner drink, or some other gesture that makes the guests feel special.

Guidelines for New Restaurants

There are specific guidelines for both new and existing restaurants that must be followed. The dining room manager should be aware of this law and the guidelines that must be followed. If the restaurant is not accessible, a plan should to put into effect to make the restaurant accessible. As an example, it has been reported that Planet Hollywood in Washington, D.C., has agreed to install a ramp leading to the front entrance, place an accessible restroom on the first floor, lower counters in the bar and retail areas, build a ramp into the science fiction theme dining area and install signage required by the ADA.

This occurred because of a complaint brought by wheelchair users Atsuko Kuwana and her husband, Michael Winter, after they had to enter through a locked side service door because the three steps leading to the front entrance allegedly were not ramped. With restaurants becoming more accessible to guests with disabilities, the host has to be aware of what can be done to make their dining experience enjoyable. The type of disability guests have will dictate their special needs as well as the consideration that the host gives them. For instance, a visually impaired guest should be led to the table and have the location of the utensils explained by the host by imagining the table as the face of a clock (e.g., the coffee cup is at five o'clock). If the guest has a seeing-eye dog, the host leads the guest to a table where the dog can lie down without being in the traffic flow.

In addition, guests must be seated in the least restrictive environment. A host cannot give people with disabilities the poorest table in the restaurant. The host would seat guests in wheel-chairs at a table that is out of the flow of traffic, but where the guest is comfortable.' The host may assist the guest in whatever way possible to make the person feel welcome. It may be necessary to move the table so the guest can position his or her wheelchair comfortably at the place setting. In some instances, it might be necessary to raise the table to a height that will accommodate wheelchairs. Regardless of the disability of the guest, the host has to remember, and impress upon the staff, that these individuals are as valuable to the restaurant as guests who are not disabled.

The staff has to be taught to treat all guests with courtesy, and to put forth extra effort so that all can enjoy themselves and have a pleasant dining experience. Unfortunately, there will be times when a guest has a complaint about the wait for the table, the food, the services, or prices. The host must know how to handle complaints and be able to resolve the situation so the guest feels that the problem has been solved satisfactorily.

6

Selection of Curtains

Curtains can be very difficult to clean and maintain. Often times they will shrink or tear easily. Also, while Dry Cleaning curtains, all pins must be removed, then put back in once the process is complete.

Curtain Making

For plain, unpatterned fabrics, texture is important - panels of raw silk or hessian weave have a whole array of textures that just add that little extra detail, while velvet curtains have the uncanny ability to change with the lighting. Bold, contrasting patterns such as stripes look good in a formal setting. Toile de jouy or floral patterns give a room a softer more relaxed. It is a good idea to have your curtains lined as this will prevent them from fading from continuous exposure to sunlight. Thicker linings can also be added to keep the heat from escaping the room—they can act as a kind of insulating layer.

Lined curtains will be significantly heavier and may require a sturdier support system. Making your own curtains enables you to colour co-ordinate your room and even match the curtains with the cushions or tablecloth if you desire. The initial idea may seem a little daunting but don't be put off. If you can use a sewing machine and sew in a straight line, making your own curtains is not difficult and can be a satisfying project. Unlined curtains with metal or plastic hooks to attach to the curtain pole are the most straightforward to make and so a good place for a beginner to start.

Measurements

When taking measurements for curtains you need to be very exact. It would be pretty disappointing to proudly hang your curtains only to find they're an inch too short. When measuring for the length of the curtains, take the measurements from the curtain pole to the bottom of the window. You need to add on 8 inches to the total height measurement to allow for hems. As you want your curtains to be gathered when shut and not pulled taught across the window, double the width measurement of your window and add 8 inches for seams to get your ideal width.

Fabric Selection

As you'll be making unlines curtains, it's important to choose good quality material in an appropriate colour. If you are making unlined curtains for a bedroom for example, you won't be thanked for making them in white. Fabrics come in two widths, 45 and 60 inches. This is wide enough to fit all standard windows; if your windows are unusually large, you might need to buy two widths and stitch them together. When purchasing the material, round up any measurements, as it's always better to have too much than too little. Cut the material in half to create the two curtain panels.

Making Process

Lay out the fabric on a flat surface with the right side facing down. Turn a double 1-inch hem at each side, pin in place, then stitch. Turn a double 3-inch hem at the bottom, and do the same. Remember to use a ruler or tape measure to ensure your measurements are accurate. A strip of heading tape into which the hooks will go needs to be sewn at the top of the curtain. The best way to attach this is to turn down 2 inches at the top, lay the heading tape on top of this and stitch both in place at the same time. The curtain hooks are then looped into the heading tape and your curtain is ready for hanging.

Glass window panes allow the light into our houses and give us a view of the outside world. However glass does not keep the heat in and also allows passersby to look in depriving us of our privacy. Window curtains have the practical function of keeping the light out and the warmth in. The most common form of window curtains are two panels which hang either side of the window frame when open and can be pulled shut to cover the whole window. Single panels cover the whole window and can be held to one side with tiebacks. The panels can be gathered or pleated at the top so they fall in folds.

Windows which have radiators under the sills should have drapes which come to just below the sill to allow the heat to circulate round the room. Floor-length window curtains look very smart but absorb the heat from radiators. Drapes with large patterns, such as toile, need to be used for large windows to avoid breaking up the interwoven pattern. Sheer curtains allow the light in and can therefore be left covering the window as a permanent fixture. Heavier materials such as velvet are a snug choice for the bedroom as they don't let the warmth flow out and they achieve a nearly complete "Blackout" state—great for light sleep.

Lighter fabrics work better in bathrooms as they are less prone to retaining moisture and going moldy. Cotton drapes work well in bathrooms, kitchens or in kids' rooms as no fuss needs to be made when it comes to washing—simply bung them in the machine on a regular wash. Bay windows consist of three window panes with the two side panes angled to form the bay. Bay window curtains are usually attached using track which has been bent to fit the window. Arched windows can also present a little difficulty. They can be fitted with clear rods shaped to fit the window which can then be used to hang a lace curtain or other decorative window treatment. For particularly awkward windows, it may be worth considering having custom curtains made.

Ready-made curtains are available in different styles and fabrics and provide an affordable and practical solution to most window dressing problems. Windows allow us to look out onto the world while bringing life and light into our homes. Using the correct window treatments can maximise the beauty of your windows; chosen well, the right curtains, blinds and window hardware lends style and atmosphere to any room. Compare how luscious velvet drapes reflect the grandness of a manor house while a beach bungalow benefits from light, airy sheers that billow with the breeze.

Bright yellow curtains cheer up a kitchen while simple black valances keep small bathrooms neutral; lace can be flirtatious while corduroy lends an earthy feeling. Curtain rods are easily hidden while curtain poles capped with end finials are decoration in themselves. Choosing the best window treatments for your home requires a little more work than simply picking the colour of a curtain.

Choosing your window treatments also means understanding and accepting the four facets of window treatment design:

— Fabric is a major decision. Not only will your fabric convey a certain attitude (i.e. velvet is much more formal than cotton) but it must be of the right weight to balance with your window.
— How you attach the window treatments to the window is also important; rods, poles and rings are all unique elements of design.
— Choosing the right heading to complement your treatment can add style and flair or cause a fashion disaster.

Finishing off your window treatments with embellishments requires a bit of design awareness; for example, you never want to make a modern window treatment appear too fussy with excess additions.

Window Treatment

Window treatment design is about more than just curtains and blinds; in fact, four elements of style are responsible for adding atmosphere and interest no matter the motif. The ability to customise each of the four elements, from the fabric and support to the heading and embellishments, allows you to control how your widow treatment impacts the room. Fabric is the most important and defining part of any window treatment. A formal dining room comes together with the addition of a pair of rich damask drapes while a sunny kitchen fares better with light cotton. When deciding on a window treatment design, be aware that fabric depends on three aspects; colour, weight and pattern.

Colour is integral to defining your design; warm and earthy shades add coziness while cool colors come across as 'crisp.' The weight of the fabric makes a different statement; heavy curtains frame an area to impart a reserved air while lighter ones billow and open up a living area. Pattern is the last aspect. Plain, textured fabrics are generally less noticeable than those that carry a design, but subtle patterns recede more than striking colors do. Support is the second element of any window treatment design.

There are a few things to consider when choosing your attachments; Analyse your fabric and verify that its weight and design matches the support; wool curtains might be too heavy for a thin track while a heavy pole can carry attention away from delicate sheers. Hidden tracks and curtain rods are generally less noticeable support while poles can be quite decorative, especially with the addition of end finials and curtain rings. Heading is considered similar to support but is truly its own individual design element. The heading controls how your fabric hangs and while concealing the support. Stiff pencil pleats and French pleats can be gathered across a curtain rod to impart fancy formality while a simple slot heading allows a curtain to slide easily across a rod.

Rings and pleats are paired for decoration while a pole adds extra flair and ruffles and eyelets are distinct in their own manner. Embellishment is the last aspect to take into account; use them to give your window treatment design that extra bit of unique flair. Embellishment ranges from simple drapes and folds in the fabric to fanciful hand-made lace borders and dangling charms. They can be purely decorative in the form of tassels, buttons and fringes, or provide function through ties, loops and tassels.

French doors are a beautiful accent to any home, infusing rooms with distinct style while bringing in light and air. It is essential to find the right French door window treatments to foster, rather than diminish, their unique appeal; however, this doesn't mean wading through stacks of curtains, rods and blinds. Here's some advice on how to dress your French doors. French doors are designed to be used. They allow access to a deck, veranda or even another room by swinging outwards or inwards on hinges. This makes finding appropriate French door window treatments a bit more difficult, as you never want to block the doorway or obstruct the hinge mechanism from functioning properly.

There are always solutions for decorating your French doors. Door panels in sheer or solid curtains are a popular choice; gather them on poles at the bottom and top of the window and then draw the fabric together in the middle to resemble an hour glass shape. This lets in a bit of light while allowing some privacy; the panels may then be drawn outwards again to cover more of the window. Thin, sheer curtains work especially well with French doors provided that they are on a curtain rod or pole long enough to hold the fabric clear of the doors. In fact, it can be quite pleasant to open a set of French doors, draw a pair of sheer curtains and allow the breeze to send them sailing breezily into the room.

If you're searching for more privacy, full-size indoor shutters on a track can be a great choice. Slide them along the tracks to open and close; when placed across French doors these wooden shutters afford maximum privacy and security. If you prefer to use window treatments that are not the same size of the doors, try a set of plantation shutters. These attractive wooden shutter tilt up and down to close are also another good option. Your neighbourhood fabric and craft store is a good place to go if you have questions about material. Visit a local home improvement store for suggestions on hardware; home furnishing stores usually carry a great assortment of shades and blinds in their window treatment departments.

Bay windows make a beautiful and unique accent to any home, but using the wrong window treatment will only diminish their natural appeal. On the other hand, the right bay window treatments will highlight, illuminate and bring the sparkle out of your window. Bay windows are unique with their three dimensional, three window design as the additional angles make it hard to find headings. Curtain rods and poles can be used, but they must be bought and installed individually in three different sets. This tends to throw a lot of designers off track. It's best to stick to simple window treatments because decorating a bay window with multiple blinds or curtains will appear fussy and overly complicated. There are a few options for bay window treatments; some people find success with a curved track that follows the angling of the window.

A single or double set of curtains can then be drawn across the continuous track. Be prepared to use power tools or to enlist extra help when choosing this option, for bending the metal curtain rod into the same shape as the window can requires a bit of manpower and/or expense. Another suggestion is to use three separate, solid shades that gather up into themselves at the top of the window. As for curtains, simple swags or Roman curtains are the best option because they can be easily affixed to each individual window. If you prefer to have long drapes, plan to install a curtain rod or pole across the top of the bay window on the wall facing into the room.

Kitchens aren't just for cooking anymore. Today they can be a stylish centerpiece, the hub of family life or even an area devoted to entertaining. As more attention is paid to their design, installing the perfect kitchen window treatments becomes essential for conveying atmosphere. Not just any old curtain or window hardware will suffice when striving for the ideal kitchen décor. Choosing your kitchen window treatments depends on the style of kitchen you have; here are the best window treatment suggestions organised by decorating theme: Country kitchens are back in vogue. Evoking a pleasant, homey feeling, country style ranges from bright and simple to cluttered and cozy. Try small floral or fruit patterns and coloured block checks in a set of tab curtains or balloon valance.

Fabrics such as muslin, cotton, canvas and woven fabrics work well. Or skip curtains altogether and place a carved wooden shelf above the window, then decorate with copper pots or garland. Celebrate sleek and modern; maximise the impact of tile and stainless steel by integrating your kitchen window treatments into your contemporary décor. Simple curtain designs are best for maintaining the 'clean' look; let in the light with sheer fabrics such as treated or raw silk and muslin. Bright primary colors and geometric patterns work well or add some texture with corduroy and canvas.

A simple pull shade will quietly blend in while a Roman shade adds decorative flair. Or affix a set of glass shelves onto the window and place a couple of clear, coloured glass objects onto them. Try cherry prints or vines and small hanging mini-drapes; finish your curtain rods and poles in lacquer and enamel. For a funky 'diner style,' hang up a pair of café curtains. Complete the look by hanging retro pictures and prints alongside the window. Old European kitchens provide a unique yet popular style. Try traditional Laura Ashley florals, ruffled valances and white shutters for an English air. Invoke the warmth and bustle of an Italian country kitchen by hanging strands of garlic and peppers in large windows.

Stick to washed out shades of warm colors. French subtlety can be conveyed through shades of white and blue, bistro curtains and brass curtain rods. Spanish influence is supplied by deep, warm colors such as maroon and burnt sienna, decorative wall tiles and embroidered panels.

DIY Patterns

Although variety is a good thing when it comes to home

decorating, even the greatest amount of choice doesn't guarantee you'll find exactly what you're looking for. On the bright side, it is relatively easy to create and prepare your own window treatment patterns, provided you keep these considerations in mind:

Complication. How difficult or simple do you want your window treatment to be? Café curtains, which are basically two pieces of fabric strung across the window at the window's midpoint, are very easy to make and only require a basic curtain rod. On the other hand, lambrequins and goblet-pleated puddle drapes demand more extensive time and effort. Keep in mind that the more involved your window treatment patterns, the more energy and money you may have to spend to accomplish the look you want.

Cost: Ask yourself how much you are planning to spend. Do your window treatment patterns involve expensive components such as fancy drapes, brass curtain rods or carved wooden finials? Pairing solid curtains with sheers doubles your cost. Adding trim and other notions also increases the amount of money you should plan to spend. Simple fabrics such as cotton and polyester blends are less expensive than richer ones and metal and wood window hardware drives up the cost more so than plastic.

Directions: Illusions of grandeur are easily shot down with the realisation that you don't understand the directions or the terminology. Make sure your chosen window treatment pattern makes it perfectly clear what you should be buying and/or doing in order to achieve your desired look. It's never a good thing when you are half done and realise that you bought a socket bracket when what you really needed was a spool rod.

Measuring: Remember the old saying, 'measure twice and cut once.' Be precise in all your measurements; many window treatment patterns purposefully require you to leave some 'extra room' for the eventual gathering or draping of the fabric. Fabric can also be one of the most expensive components of the window treatment; cutting corners when measuring will only result in you cutting the material incorrectly.

Sometimes having too many choices can be more frustrating than not having enough. The wide array of window decorating options and accessories can be mind-boggling, yet even a wide assortment of goods doesn't guarantee you'll find exactly what you're looking for. If you're stumped for decorating ideas, it can be a good idea to look into custom window treatments. Whoever said all windows are created equal? Many people order custom window treatments to cover oddly shaped or hard-to-fit windows. Others simply want their decorating schemes to remain unique.

Of course, it's always hassle-free to leave your window treatment responsibilities to the experts. No matter your reasoning, it's easy to order custom measured and designed window treatments; all you need to know is where to look. A number of companies offer custom window treatments. Not only can customers specify their own dimensions, but they may choose from among a wide variety of additional features such as remote-controlled shades, special tinting and cordless blinds. Simply contact one of the following stores to talk to a designer, order a free brochure or catalogue, or to visit a store in person.

Kinds of Curtains

Bamboo Curtains: Bring the spirit of aloha into your home with hand-painted bamboo curtains. As a souvenir of a magical vacation in Hawaii, or simply a style choice, bamboo curtains are an attractive accessory in any home. What's so great about this material is that it is an environmentally-friendly, and because bamboo grows very quickly it is a realistically replenish able resource. This beautiful, lightweight material is ideal for attractive curtains all round the house. People use them as door curtains, window curtains, wall hangings or put them over a closet instead of doors.

Bamboo curtains are not commonplace and are often only stocked by specialist vendors. Bamboo curtains bring a touch of the tropics into your home. Their Hawaiian origins are reflected in some of the designs available: a crouched surfer riding a wave, a palm tree in front of a setting sun. The curtains are made of pieces of bamboo which are about half inch wide and are stuck together to form a surface for hand-painting or printing a design on. They are attached to a wooden slat which runs across the top and has eyelets to make the curtains easy to put up.

Other designs that would appeal to children in particular are available such as mermaids or animals such as cats or dolphins. *Beaded bamboo curtains*: Long, cylindrical bamboo beads are strung together on threads and attached to a wooden slat across the top. Bamboo is easy to dye and different-coloured beads are used on the strands to form a pattern. As bamboo is lightweight it is a good material for making door curtains. The hollow beads make a knocking noise as they are moved by the wind or by someone brushing through the strands aside - an unobtrusive and somewhat calming sound. Installing bamboo curtains is not a complicated process as they are usually attached to a wood frame with eyelets.

Hold up the frame and make sure it is level above the door or window where it is to go. It is better to do it by eye in case the door or window frame is not completely level. Mark where the curtain hooks need to go with a pencil and then hammer in the hooks in. The curtain eyelets should fit over hooks. You may need to trim your curtain to fit the doorway or window. Trim carefully—do not take too much off, if you take too little off you can always trim some more off but once you have gone too far you can not stick it back on!

Toile Curtains: Toile curtains are a popular choice for a peaceful, rustic look in your home. Toile refers to the pattern used on the material and toile was first produced in the French town of Jouy in the 18th century. Therefore toile can also be referred to as toile de jouy. Plants, animals, flowers and country scenes such as deer drinking out of rivers were printed on cotton fabric. Originally the designs would use just one colour on a plain background but later on multicoloured designs started appearing.

French toile curtains usually have a coloured pattern in colors such as red, blue or green on a white or cream background but there are some unusual variations available such as a red pattern on a gold background. Toile curtains are produced in different fabrics these days including plastic—yes you even get "toiled" shower curtains! French toile curtains add peace and charm to a bedroom or kitchen. The style of pattern is not intrusive and goes with most types rustic / country themed decor. Remember when using patterned fabric that a large pattern on a small window won't be seen properly—it will appear broken up and "bitsy".

This type of pattern consists of scenes that need to be seen as a whole to make sense and would therefore suit a large space such as floor-length curtains for French windows. Another consideration is whether you would like the drapes lined or not. Sheer curtains allow the light through which shows the pattern up but lined toile curtains allow the design to be seen more clearly. The other advantage of lined curtains is that the lining prevents the pattern from fading in the sun.

Sheer Curtains: Sheer curtains are translucent drapes which cover a window while allowing the maximum amount light to still stream through, meaning the curtains can be kept closed. Their purpose is to screen largely to add "some" privacy while not cutting the room off from any beauty emanating in from the outside. Sheer drapes are made of fine, delicate fabric so they allow daylight into the room while ensuring privacy. Any sort of open-weave fabric will fulfill this purpose—net or lace curtains are popular in most suburban homes. A great alternative for those who want plain drapes without any pattern or frills is muslin, a thin fabric made of cotton.

Printed muslin is also available—for instance white muslin with a white printed pattern such as a fleur de lis looks particularly striking. Plain muslin is translucent and the printed pattern is opaque so the pattern shows up when the sun is shining. Other popular materials include voile which often contains silk—making it a slightly pricier option—yet one that can add a natural softness to any room. Layering and combining different shades (printed and plain) can result in some of the most magnificent and dramatic effects being created.

Experiment with having sheer drapes in two or more different colors, say plain white underneath and fuchsia pink sheer curtains over the top—the combination will shut out more light but still be translucent enough to give a glowing effect through the curtains. Sheer curtains can either be the sole window dressing or can be supplemented with heavier curtains or blinds - possibly in the event when the need for privacy overshadows the need for natural light.

Lace Curtains: Lace curtains are an attractive window covering which let the light into the room while shutting out unsightly views or the gaze of people passing by. Lace is an open-weave fabric which is made by looping, knotting or plaiting fine threads together to form intricate, delicate patterns. Sheer curtains made of lace have the ability to add a romantic, traditional feel to most rooms. A single lace panel can have a permanent position hung across a window and be coupled with heavier outer curtains which can drawn to provide additional cover at night-time. Lace curtains can be backed with sheer, coloured linings to create interesting effects.

Lace-making originated in north Italy in the sixteenth century—Venice, in particular, was a center for lace-making. Hand-made lace took a lot of work to produce and was worn as status symbol. Motifs or designs were created which could then be stitched on to netting or another patterned open-weave background. Techniques for making lace include crocheting, needlepoint or machine. Modern lace is made of linen, cotton, rayon, polyester or other man-made materials.

Net Curtains : Net curtains are made from fabric with an open weave pattern which is usually a netting pattern, as the name suggests. They are usually white or cream and usually used as an under curtain with heavier curtains that can be drawn over the top. They stay over the window all the time and are not raised, removed or drawn. Ready made net curtains are readily available over the Net or from department stores. White won't fade in the sunshine - and is probably the most popular choice. Net curtains are the suburban choice for keeping nosy neighbours out while allowing the light in. Interior fashion has never moved away from the need for bright airy rooms and net curtains can help achieve this feel.

Net window curtains can be made of voile, cotton, muslin or nylon. The cheapest ones are made of nylon. Muslin panels are an alternative to net window curtains. Muslin is a flimsy plain cotton fabric which makes an ideal window dressing. Nets can either have a plain net-like pattern or have motifs and more elaborate patterns interwoven—similar to those found in lace. These need to be hand-washed—they are quite delicate so it is best not to put them in a machine. There are detergents designed for brightening net curtains on the market—this stops and repairs any discolouring. Net curtains can look quite drab after a while and they do collect dust so they should be washed regularly.

Beaded Curtains: Popularised in the trendy, colourful 1960s, beaded curtains have been decorating walls, windows and doorways for almost half a century. Traditionally used to separate rooms, camouflage closets, hide doors and increase privacy, beaded curtains have also made an appearance as part of the Asian 'feng-shui' decorating scheme. Beaded curtains made a comeback when the Asian decorating scheme of feng-shui soared in popularity. Designed to balance your life energy (or 'chi') by reorganising your living space, feng-shui uses these curtains as room dividers, designed to slow down the passage of your chi throughout your home. Most curtains measure 36" by 72", which fits the dimensions for a standard doorway. If a doorway is larger that , it's easy to hang multiple curtains side by side.

Kid's Curtains: Kids curtains brighten up any child's room, adding fun flair to any decorating scheme. Long gone are the days of boring old fabric; today kids curtains come in a wide assortment of colors, themes and zany patterns. Try to stick to shorter curtains such as valances and café curtains rather than floor-length drapes when outfitting your child's bedroom or playroom; this makes it easier to vacuum the floor without having to worry about sucking up the curtains. Keeping the curtains short prevents younger children from reaching, hanging on, or tearing down the material. It is also less likely that your child will trip over a short curtain when running around.

Relatively inexpensive and machine washable, cotton is the preferred fabric when choosing kids curtains. Smudgy fingers and crumbs often gravitate to everything in a young child's path, so try to refrain from hanging flimsy, expensive fabrics in your child's windows. When choosing curtains, keep in mind that kids grow quickly, resulting in constantly changing likes and dislikes. What your child prefers at age seven will probably be completely different from what he or she wants a year later.

A good tip to keep in mind when choosing and budgeting for any child's décor is to avoid trends, which can rapidly lose favour. Try to choose a style that is sure to stick around for some time; for example, decorating with trendy cartoon characters or the latest hot pop group can backfire if they lose popularity. Kids curtains come in such a wide variety of styles that it is nearly impossible not to find something to suit both parent and child.

Try curtains printed with ballerinas for your little dancer, classic cartoon characters for your budding film critic and sports teams for the future athlete. Younger children might benefit from an alphabet or circus theme, which allow for any colour choice. Of course, any set of kids curtains are livened up with fun accessories; use baseball bats instead of curtain rods for a sports-theme room or hang a pair of ballet slippers or a cowboy hat on the end of the curtain rod.

Curtain Valances

Curtain valances cover the top of the curtains and hide unsightly tracks or fixtures. Curtain pelmets are a stiff, fixed cover which runs out from the wall and across the top of the curtains while valances are single short panels which attach to the curtain pole or track in the same way as the main drapes. They go across the top of the window for decoration and consist of one single piece of material or panel which stays in place whether the main curtains are open or closed. Usually curtains and valances are bought together as a matching set but it can be worth experimenting contrasting materials, colors and styles to create a unique look.

There are different styles of curtain valances. Panel valances are plain, short panels which attach to the curtain pole. Panels can be gathered or shirred for decoration. Shirred panels are where the material is gathered in parallel rows. The bottom hem doesn't have to be straight; it can either be longer in the middle or shorter to make the bottom curved. One alternative to curtain valances or pelmets is swag. This is where a panel is draped across the curtain rod so it dips in the middle and the ends are pleated or gathered so they fall in folds down the sides. Box valances go around the top area of the window - ie comes out from the wall, across the top of the window and back towards the wall the other side to create a box shape.

There is a type of curtain track with a clip on valance track which comes out in front of the main track. The valance attaches to the valance track and hides the track holding the curtain on the wall. Another method of attaching valances is to use medallion holdbacks or tiebacks which screw onto the wall and two curtain rods can be fitted to them, one for the valance and one for the main curtain.

Use of Curtain Tiebacks

Curtain tiebacks are used for holding drapes back from the window to allow more light in and to stop the curtains blowing around on a windy day. In addition to tucking the curtains out of the way when they are open, tiebacks are also an attractive window finishing. Tiebacks made out of the same fabric as the curtains are usually bought with the curtains as part of a matching set. Tassel curtain tiebacks are made of threads braided into a rope with tassels on the end. They are usually available in a range of colors so that you can either match your curtains or pick a contrasting colour.

Traditionally tiebacks are positioned two thirds of the way down the curtain so the hooks to hold the tieback in place are screwed about half way down the length of the wall. However you can have a curtain tieback around the center of the curtain or attached to the curtain rod, pulling the curtain back from about a third of the way down. You would need to use longer tiebacks to achieve this effect. Ornamental wooden or metal tiebacks screw into the wall next to the window and the curtain can be tucked behind.

Metal curtain tiebacks are available in different finishes such as brass, bronze or iron and finials are attached to the end for decoration. Wrought iron tiebacks have striking designs and are sculptured into detailed patterns. If the curtains are plain, you can get away with ornate, unusual tiebacks which are a feature in their own right. Finials can be attached the ends of plain metal tiebacks for decoration. These can be bought to match the finials on the end of the curtain pole. Antique tiebacks from the Victorian age were designed like a door knob with a metal plate that screwed into the wall or window frame and a long pin with a flower (or other design) for the head made of glass or wood.

Rods

Curtains are supported using either curtain rods or track depending on what sort of fitting the window or door lends itself to. Rods, or curtain poles, are the more attractive form of curtain support and can add to the decor. Track is the cheaper option but looks unsightly and should be covered if possible. If there is not enough space above the window for a curtain rod, then track has to be used instead. There are many different styles of curtain rod on the market, so finding a style in keeping with your home should not be a problem. Plain wooden or metal poles can be dressed up with exotic finials and vice versa.

Impressive wrought-iron poles with old-fashioned designs, such as a fleur de lis, look almost medieval.

Metal curtain rods with a shiny brass finish look very smart. Consider the rest of the room and the curtains when choosing a curtain pole.

Rings and Finials: The poles should come with matching rings which slide onto the pole and have smaller metal rings hanging from them. The curtains have hooks threaded through the back of the curtain and can be attached to the curtain rings using these. Both the poles and the rings are visible. The poles can be finished off with curtain finials which slide on the end of the poles to stop the end rings falling off and for decoration.

Finials can be mixed and matched so you can have a plain pole with an ornate finial or an intricately-designed pole with a plain finial. Often curtain rods and finials are bought as a matching set. While curtain rods are usually bought with matching curtain rings, it can be fun experimenting with contrasting rings. Remember that the rings should be at least half an inch larger in diameter than the pole. Another option is to have the curtain stitched so the top hem forms a pocket big enough for the rod to fit through. Tab top curtains have wide straps sewn across the top of the curtains which attach the curtain to the pole. Curtain rings are most the most common method and have the advantage that curtains can easily be taken down and put up without moving the curtain rod.

Fitting curtain rods to bay windows: Bay windows consist of three windows to fit in the three-sided bay; usually bay windows use flexible track which bends around the bay for curtains. However for older bay windows with thicker gaps between the panes, you can use curtain rods and still not lose too much light when the curtains are pulled back. You need one rod per window and the middle curtain will pull across to one side. Using tiebacks can help hold the curtain out of the pane. If there is not much room between the top of the window and the ceiling then using curtain poles may not be possible.

Double curtain rods: These have two parallel rods projecting from one set of brackets to allow for a curtain valance or having two layers of drapes. People may wish to have two layers of curtains if they want to have a thinner under layer which can be drawn to allow the light in but cover an unsightly view or stop people looking in. The outer curtains would be heavier curtains which could be drawn at night-time. The other alternative is to have two sets of sheer drapes to create unusual effects with light and colour.

Installation

Curtain poles are an attractive alternative to using track to support your curtains and are usually exposed, meaning that there is often call for some decorative flair to blend them into the feel of the room. They come in all sorts of styles and materials from plain simple poles to unusual, intricately-designed poles. They can only be fitted if there is enough space above the window—hence track is usually used for bay windows. Curtain poles are attached to the wall, window frame or ceiling with brackets. Where the poles are fitted depends on how strong the supporting wall is. If the wall is soft and uneven it may be better to attach the curtain pole to the window frame which is likely to hold better.

Another alternative would be to attach the pole to the ceiling. Remember it is not only the weight of the curtain pole that is an issue; the weight of the curtains needs to be taken into consideration as well. The pole should be positioned about 4-6 inches above the window frame and if there is space either side of the window, then the pole should extend beyond the edge of the window frame to allow the curtains to be pulled back away from the window.

Mark where the brackets should go in a soft pencil and then install the brackets according to the manufacturer's instructions. This usually involves drilling holes for screws. Fix one of the brackets and, attach the curtain pole and then fix the other bracket. Put one curtain ring on each end of the pole outside the bracket before attaching the curtain finials. This is to prevent any chance of the outside edge of the curtain being pulled across the window area.

Tension curtain rods use a spring to hold the rod in place i.e. there is no need for brackets, drilling or screws. These rods are more practical and would work best with a window treatment that hides the rod—for instance panel drapes with a pocket hem that the rod slides into. Double curtain poles for hanging two layers of drapes consist of two poles attached to a single bracket and should be installed in the same way as single curtain rods.

Working with brackets: Curtain rod brackets are used for fixing the rods or poles which will be used to support the curtains to the wall. Usually brackets are bought with the curtain pole to ensure they fit the pole correctly and match the rod's colour or style. However it is possible to purchase brackets, finials and curtain rings separately—and work towards creating a more personal look. Curtain rod brackets are fitted into the wall, window frame or ceiling depending on what is going to give the best support. Wall fittings are the most common but if the wall is too soft to support the weight of the pole and the curtains, then consider screwing the brackets into the window frame or the ceiling.

For recess windows you can get brackets that slot over the end of the pole in matching colors and styles so they are less noticeable. Alternatively use wooden brackets with a U shape for the rod to slot into and paint the wood the same shade as the wall so it blends in. When installing the brackets, it is important to follow the manufacturers' instructions as different designs require different set of procedures. Wooden brackets usually have a metal plate that is screwed on to the wall and then the bracket screws on to the plate. When deciding where to place the brackets, use a steel tape measure to measure the correct distance and use a soft pencil to mark where the holes should be drilled. Space should be allowed either side of the window so the curtains can be pulled back away from the window frame.

Discount Curtains : Many people are surprised to find that one of the most expensive accessories when decorating a window is the curtain itself. It's true; even a little bit of fabric can be expensive once it's tailored, hemmed and packaged for sale as a curtain. But with a little knowledge and a set of discount curtains, anyone can outfit a house without going broke.

Curtains vary so dramatically in price, style and quality that anyone can find what they want while still remaining cost conscious. Remember that the more area you need the more money you should plan to spend. For example, long panels and drapes can be more expensive than short shades and valances. How much cash is required also depends on the type of fabric you plan to hang in your window. Velvets, wools, brocades and other lush fabrics can be very pricy.

On the other hand, silk, crepes and sheers can also require quite a bit of money. Your best bet when searching for low prices is to turn to simple fabrics such as cotton, polyester and percale blends. Keep in mind, however, that these fabrics are more prone to fading when exposed to sunlight. Cost also increases when embellishments, embroidery and other decorative aspects are added. If you know how to work a sewing machine, or simply consider yourself crafty, sometimes the best discount curtains are the ones you make yourself. Buying raw fabric is cheaper than buying finished curtains; all it takes is some concentration and a sewing needle to cut and hem them to size.

7

Carpet Maintenance

Care should be taken when mopping or refinishing hard surface floors that butt-up to carpet in order not to contaminate the carpet edge. Walk-off mats should be considered for use in these potential trouble spots. Because carpet is the only textile product which must withstand people walking on it continually, it is extremely important that a maintenance plan be in place for every carpet installation. Although consumers would never think about buying an automobile and not taking care of it (clean-up, routine maintenance, and repairs), it's a common belief that all that has to be done to carpet is to vacuum it. Let's compare carpet maintenance to maintenance of hard surface materials.

End-users are fully aware that hard surface must be stripped and polished at recommended intervals. They also understand that after this stripping, polishing, and sealing, people are kept off the surface for a specified amount of time. Carpet deserves the same respect. Carpet must be vacuumed routinely and extracted at regular intervals. It must be allowed to dry completely before people walk on it. Additionally the mill applied fluorchemical protection must be maintained, and should be tested following each extraction to determine if reapplication is necessary to maintain the effectiveness of the soil resistance, this treatment must be allowed to "cure" before new soil is tracked into the area.

There are three key maintenance areas to be considered:

— preventative maintenance,

— interim maintenance, and

— restorative maintenance.

CARPET SELECTION

The appearance of carpet depends upon several factors—

— colour,

— pattern,

— density,

— fiber, and

— a viable carpet maintenance programme.

Colour selection is very important. Lighter coloured carpet shows soil more readily and requires more attention to maintain a high level of appearance. In locations where the soil colour is dark, darker colours of carpet tend to help mask tracked-in soil. In areas where soil is red in colour, a redder hue of carpet will show less soil. However, light colored carpet can be used near shore and beach areas where sand is prevalent. Darker colored carpet in this case will show sand-colored footprints. Carpeting for restaurants should be in a bold pattern or pronounced tweed. Whatever the case, the carpet will look better and require less attention if the carpet colour and soil colour are compatible.

Density is important in determining how well the carpet will perform and maintain its appearance. If the carpet is made with a loose, lightweight construction, soil can penetrate around the face fibers and down to the backing. The abrasive action of the soil can cut through the fibers, and the soil particles at the base become difficult to remove. A correctly constructed carpet for commercial use is made with the face fibers packed in tightly. Most of the tracked-in soil stays on the surface of a densely constructed carpet where it can be vacuumed away easily.

Carpet with a *sculptured pattern* will require more frequent maintenance in order for the carpet to retain its sculptured appearance. This should be considered at the time the carpet is selected because more frequent vacuuming and pile lifting will be required in order to maintain the pattern definition of the carpet.

The type of fiber in the carpet should be considered, whether it's a man-made fiber, or a natural fiber like wool. More than 90% of all carpet produced today is manufactured with man-made fibers. Man-made fibers and wools require different types of detergents. Be sure of the fiber content of the carpet before you start any cleaning procedures. The following procedures for effective carpet maintenance have been developed from practical experience and have proven successful when used in conjunction with carpet of appropriate fiber, construction, and colour.

The appropriate selection of carpet colour and construction in addition to the professionalism to establish a proper maintenance programme and the discipline to carry it through will create satisfied carpet users. The use of all cleaning chemicals must be in accordance with proper safety practices, rules, and regulations. The suitability of the products, chemicals, equipment, methods, and procedures for an intended use shall be the responsibility of the user.

Each component of the carpet maintenance system, vacuuming, spotting, and cleaning, must have a positive impact on the indoor air quality; a negative impact is not acceptable. The carpet maintenance procedure selected for any building should be that system which will not adversely impact the interior environment. The products and systems utilised in carpet maintenance must have very low total volatile organic emissions, which will dissipate rapidly. All equipment must be safe in operation. The system must be capable of safely removing the foreign contaminants which are brought against the carpet in normal service conditions. This includes tracked-in soil, indoor allergens, airborne dust, solids, liquids, or gasses that have contaminated carpet. The carpet maintenance systems and products selected must not distort or damage the carpet face fibers, dyes, texture appearance, or backing system.

Maintenance Programme

The maintenance programme is no less important than the initial carpet specification itself. It used to be that carpet was allowed to soil heavily, almost to the point of no return, before something was done. Research and field testing have revealed that this antiquated approach to carpet cleaning allows abrasive soil particles to build up in the carpet. This shortens the wearlife and abrades synthetic carpet yarns causing the carpet to look much darker and/or dull in those areas, allows spills and stains to remain too long where they become difficult to remove, and diminishes the overall appearance of the carpet. We are no longer maintaining all areas of our buildings strictly for aesthetics, but are cleaning for a more healthy environment. We now spend the majority of our time living and working indoors. Public buildings and health care facilities especially must be considerate of the most hypersensitive person entering these structures.

Carpet cleaning is past history. Taking its place is a new contemporary approach to keep carpet clean, dry, and healthy. Clean carpet looks better, lasts longer and provides great performance. Today, modern carpet maintenance programming eliminates problems by starting maintenance earlier, performing maintenance operations on a more frequent but less time-consuming schedule, and thereby retaining the carpet's appearance. Remember that one of the advantages of carpet over hard surface is that carpet tends to localise soil. It catches the soil where it occurs, providing a healthier flooring surface. Therefore, considerable time and money can be saved by a programme of planned maintenance in those areas known in advance to be subject to heavier soiling.

Vacuuming

The amount of vacuuming performed should be in direct proportion to the amount and location of traffic. Areas near entryways, lobbies, elevators, and ground floors are considered heavy soiling areas and require more frequent vacuuming. By spending more time on heavily-trafficked areas with a vacuum programme, less soil is tracked farther into the building. Vacuum heavily-trafficked areas with regularity, even if soil is not visible. Carpet vacuums must be capable of removing the dry soil without producing unacceptable pile distortion and without distribution of the particulate or volatile organic chemicals into the air. High-Efficiency Particulate Air (HEPA) Filters are capable of filtering particles down to micron, which includes bacteria and spores but not viruses. These HEPA-filtered vacuums have a very healthy impact upon indoor air quality.

The upright vacuum machine with brush action is effective for soil removal. The action of the brush agitates the pile surface of the carpet and brushes soil from the fibers. The vacuum motor then removes the soil from the carpet. The presence of an adhesive carpet installation system presents a unique situation. The resultant inability of the carpet to move up to the vacuum cleaner head requires that the cleaner head be able to move down to the carpet. Such installations must be vacuumed with a "carpet groomer" agitator. This agitator has rows of brushes rather than a brush and a beater bar.

The larger the area, the larger the vacuum needed. Larger vacuums will get the job done quicker. There are many heavy-duty, large vacuums available that are designed for large areas of carpet. In addition, smaller commercial machines will be needed for areas where the large machine won't go, such as private offices, and conference rooms. Vacuum bags should be emptied frequently, and never allowed to become more than one-quarter full. As bags fill up, vacuum efficiency decreases. When vacuuming heavy traffic areas, bags should be checked and emptied often. Extra heavy traffic areas such as lobbies, entryways, and areas subjected to immediate off-the-street traffic should be vacuumed one to three times daily depending on the weather. Vacuum frequency can be determined by visual inspection. Frequent vacuuming in the heavy traffic areas will localise soil. This minimises the amount of soil being tracked into the interior of the building. Heavy Commercial (H.C.) Heavy traffic areas should be vacuumed daily, more if necessary as determined by inspection. Moderate Commercial (M.C.) Moderate traffic areas should be vacuumed daily.

Lifting Spots

The lifting of spots from the carpet surface will impact the aesthetics of the total carpet area more than any other single factor. Spots should be lifted immediately. Before attempting to remove a spot or clean a carpet, a pH test should be made on the stained area, and the water and the detergent solution. Testing for pH determines the amount of acid or alkali in soil, water, detergent, and/or chemicals. The reference numbers run from 1 to 14 with 7 being neutral. Anything below 7 is on the acidic side; anything above 7 is on the alkaline side. For instance, white vinegar usually has a reading below a pH of 1; however, it will not burn you. A stronger acid such as sulfuric or muriatic acid can cause considerable damage. The other side of the scale (7 to 14) is relatively safe up to a reading of 10.

Products with a pH above 10 and up to 14 (lye and caustic soda) become highly alkaline. These products can cause burns to humans and total destruction to the carpet. Since most of the soil in carpet is acidic, detergents are usually alkaline, cleaning solutions with pH range of 4.5-8.5 is safe for wool fiber. A pH no greater than 9 is safe for stain resist nylon, and must be anionic, nonionic or combinations thereof. Do not use cationic cleaning agents. How do you determine the pH factor? Swimming pool and aquarium supply stores usually sell pH testing kits. The kit consists of Hydron paper and a chart that is colour coded. In order to determine the pH of a spot on the carpet, wet the area to be tested with water that is neutral.

With a plastic spatula press the Hydron paper to the base of the pile. If the stain or carpet is on the acid side, use an alkaline detergent. If the stain on the carpet is on the alkaline side, use an acid spotter. If your test indicates the carpet is highly alkaline (above 10), use a slightly acidic detergent solution (pH of 4.5-6). Do not go below that reading. To continue to add alkaline to alkaline or acid to acid could cause considerable damage to the carpet. In fact, there have been numerous carpets ruined in this manner. Spills and spots should be attended to as soon as possible. The longer contaminants remain on the carpet fibers, the harder and more difficult the spots or stains are to remove.

Spot cleaning is an important phase of the overall maintenance programme, and when correctly performed, will provide an even, overall appearance to the carpet.

Place emphasis on actually removing the spot during the process. Keep the carpet as dry as possible. If loosened too quickly with too much liquid, the foreign matter can run down man-made hydrophobic fibers deeper into the pile. Spots should be removed daily. Stains differ from spots in that a stain results in a chemical reaction between the soiling material and the carpet face yarn.

Some substances, such as acids and strong oxidising agents, may cause such a severe chemical reaction with the carpet pile that they damage, or even destroy the dyes and face yarn. If the carpet installation is large, a special technician may be required for the spot removal programme. This is especially true in health care facilities where the frequency and types of spills are more varied than any other type of carpet installation. Immediate attention to spots and spills keeps the carpet looking newer longer. Commercial spot cleaning kits are available with several types of spotting agents, detergents, sponges, and brushes. You can also make up your own spot cleaning kit.

Since most of the carpet being used today is of man-made fibers, most spills can be removed with a solution of ¼ teaspoon of a liquid dishwashing detergent per 1-cup lukewarm water or Host absorbent compound cleaner. Oil or grease tracked in from the street or parking lot can be removed with a safety solvent. Caution should be exercised to avoid overwetting. Spot removal solutions and a procedure chart are covered in detail on p. 7-10. If the spill is a soft drink which contained sweetener, the area should be rinsed with a solution of 50% water, 50% white vinegar, then blotted.

After blotting, place a stack of white paper towels at least ½ an inch thick over the area and cover with a weight. Capillary action will cause the residue left in the carpet to wick up into the paper towels. This last step is especially helpful when removing spots which reappear following cleaning. The Host compound works well as a blotter.

Locate the spot by name on the spot removal chart. Remove all excess. Scrape up solids with a spatula. Blot up liquids. Do not rub. Apply spot cleaning agents with sponge or white cotton toweling in order listed. Blot with absorbent material or white cotton toweling after each application. When the spot is removed, blot up as much moisture as possible. Place a thick (1/2") layer of white paper towels over the area and weight them down with a heavy object. When the carpet is dry, vacuum to restore the texture. Each of the spot removal materials listed are identified on the spot removal chart by number.

Spot removal is a precise science. Many spots, if addressed immediately and correctly, are easily removed. Coke, coffee, gum, and mud fall into this category. More difficult spots to remove would be nail polish, shoe polish, auto greases, urine, and aged spots. Spots that only a professional cleaner should attempt, either due to the hazardous nature of the required chemicals needed to remove the spot or the permanent damage that improper techniques might produce in the carpet are rust, paints, flooding, medicines, ink, furniture stains, and dyes. Flooding voids manufacturer's warranties.

The following are the procedures of spotting:

— Test the spotting products to be used on a scrap piece of carpet first. If no carpet scrap is available, test in an inconspicuous area. Allow test area to completely dry; then check for any colour change before proceeding. If there is a colour change, do not continue. Pretest additional products until a safe spotting agent is found or call a professional cleaning technician.

— Remove any dry spill with the use of a spotting brush and bone spatula to scrape up the dry residue. (This process is very efficient for mud, mustard, and ketchup.) Then dry vacuum the area.

— Blot up wet spills immediately with a white absorbent cotton cloth, a layer of white paper towels, or an absorbent dry cleaning compound.

The general rule is that unless you know the origin of the stain and have determined that a wet spotter is required, you should always start with a nonflammable dry cleaning solvent (available through a janitorial supply company.) Work from the outer edge of the spot toward the center to avoid enlarging the spot. Never pour any dry cleaning solvent—or any other liquid cleaner—directly onto the carpet as this causes penetration into the carpet back which can produce buckling and deterioration of the backing system.

Rather, pour a small amount of solvent on the white cotton toweling and then gently apply to the spot. Blot the area with a dry white cotton cloth (or paper towels.) Work the spot by alternately moistening and blotting. When there is no longer any transfer of the spot substance to the cloth, allow the area to dry thoroughly. If any of the spot remains after using the dry cleaning solvent, then work the spot with a wet spotter (e.g., 3M, Host, Bane-Clene, ChemSpec, ServiceMaster, or Tonka Mills) using the same moistening and blotting procedures. Carefully follow the manufacturer's instructions.

Follow the same steps as you did with the dry cleaning solvent. When the stain has been removed, completely rinse the area with tap water to remove spotting agents and any residue. In some carpet colours a slight "white halo" may remain. Immediately vacuum with wet/dry vacuum. Blot with a stack of white paper towels until the moisture is absorbed. Most heavy liquid spills will work their way back to the carpet pile surface because the carpet back can act as a reservoir for the spill. Sometimes a spot will return even after it has been removed. This is due to some of the contaminant being left on the carpet back and wicking back to the surface.

Or the spotting material has not been rinsed out leaving a sticky residue that collects soil and causes the spot to return. The return of a spot following removal is no reflection on the carpet. Retreating these types of spills and thoroughly rinsing with clear water will eventually eliminate their return.

Chemical Stain: Stains differ from spots. Spots on the carpet are generally a contaminant, or foreign substance that can usually be removed, substantially or completely, by utilising sound spotting techniques. Stains are almost without exception chemicals that have altered or destroyed the carpet dyes, face yarn, or backing material. For example, Benzoyl Peroxide is generally found in acne medications and foot powders. Benzoyl Peroxide requires moisture as a catalyst to trigger the oxidation process. In climates having extended dry seasons, the stain may not appear for months.

High humidity provides sufficient moisture to start the oxidation. Carpet cleaning naturally will do the same. These stains will range in colour from yellow to orange and grow lighter in aging as the carpet dyes are further oxidised. Strong acids are capable of destroying the carpet face yarn and permanently changing the carpet colour.

Bleaches: The chlorine bleaches commonly used in the home and office (5.25-6.00% sodium hypochlorite), even in very diluted forms, will bleach many carpet dyes. Swimming pool chemicals will produce the same stripping action.

Others: Plant foods, urine, oven cleaners, toilet bowl cleaners, dyes, inks, drain cleaners, mildew removers, insecticides, foot powders, and medicines, are all capable of producing permanent and destructive carpet stains. With the exception of the volatile solvent, all other spotting agents must be completely rinsed from the carpet face yarn as the last step before drying.

Encore® SD Ultima®

One of the outstanding features of Encore® SD Ultima® is that the extrusion process creates fibers with locked-in color resulting in excellent fastness properties. Although Encore® SD Ultima® can be cleaned successfully with general spot cleaning procedures, maintenance personnel—when it is necessary—can use recommended bleach solutions to remove stains which might otherwise be impossible to remove with general spot cleaning techniques. However, a word of caution is in order: A little bleach goes a long way. Only mild solutions should be used; that is, bleach should be diluted with four parts water per one part household chlorine bleach (5.25-6.00% sodium hypochlorite), and this solution should be left on the carpet only as long as it takes to remove the stain. The following are the procedures:

— Before attempting to remove the stain, it's important to first test the spotting products to be used on a scrap piece of carpet. If no scrap is available, test an inconspicuous area. Allow the test area to dry completely, then check for any colour change before proceeding. If there is a colour change, do not continue.

— Any spill which has dried (e.g., mustard or ketchup) should be removed with the use of a spotting brush and bone spatula by scraping up the dry residue. Then follow the steps listed below and dry vacuum the area.

— Blot up wet spills with a white absorbent cloth, a layer of white paper towels, or an absorbent compound, e.g., Host compound.

— The general rule is that unless you know the origin of the stain and have determined that a wet spotter is required, you should always start with a nonflammable dry cleaning solvent (available through a janitorial supply company). Work from the outer edge of the spot toward the center to avoid enlarging the spot. Never pour any dry cleaning solvent—or any other liquid cleaner—directly onto the carpet as this causes penetration into the carpet back which can produce buckling and deterioration of the backing system. Rather, pour a small amount of solvent on the cloth and then gently apply to the spot. Blot the area with a dry white cotton cloth (or white paper towels). Work the spot by alternately moistening and blotting. When there is no longer any transfer of the spot substance to the cloth, allow the area to dry thoroughly. Use the pretested wet spotter in the same moisten and blot technique used with the dry solvent.

— If a spot or spill remains after step 4, spray with the 4:1 bleach solution. Thoroughly wet the face yarn; however, be careful not to use so much liquid that it saturates the backing. Allow to dry, generally 8 hours.

— After the area is dry repeat step 5 if the spot or spill is still evident.

— When the stain has been removed, completely rinse the area with tap water to remove spotting agents and bleach residue. In some carpet colours, a slight "white halo" may remain. Immediately vacuum with a wet/dry vacuum. Blot with a stack of white paper towels until moisture is absorbed.

Short-term Maintenance

Short-term maintenance should involve either Host absorbent compound cleaning traffic lanes and blending into surrounding clean carpet or spray cleaning the carpet surface utilising a maximum 200 RPM rotary floor machine equipped with a drive block assembly and carpet cleaning pad. A fine mist of carpet spray cleaner is applied to the carpet prior to cleaning. Dry time is 20-30 minutes. Traffic Lane Maintenance is a very important factor in the interim carpet maintenance category. After the carpet has been used for a period of time, definite traffic patterns start to appear in traffic areas. The carpet looks dull, and this dullness is caused by some types of oily soil that cling tightly to the fibers, too tightly in fact, to be removed by regular vacuuming.

These traffic lanes should be restored to the same brightness and appearance of the surrounding carpet. Carpet spray cleaning or Host (an absorbent dry cleaning compound made of small organic particles impregnated with water, detergents, and solvents), is applied to the carpet in the areas to be restored. A special machine is used to brush the compound into the carpet. The brushing action removes soil from the carpet fibers, and the soil attaches itself to the compound particles which are then vacuumed away. The results—the area can be restored by cleaning the traffic lanes and blending the traffic lane edges into the surrounding carpet, by spray cleaning, or absorbent dry cleaning. The Host system is recommended for cut pile or sculptured pattern carpet. Do not spray clean cut pile constructions.

Curative Maintenance

Restorative maintenance procedures consist of pile lifting, pre-spraying spots and heavily soiled areas, hot water extraction, or Host Absorbent extraction, and re-application of carpet protector. Maximum allowable dry time for any maintenance procedure is 8 hours. The two factors that dictate cleaning frequencies are the type of use, (i.e., office, school, healthcare), and the traffic classification. These two factors will dictate the frequency of maintenance procedures from vacuuming to overall cleaning. There is no one cleaning system that fits all facility requirements. Some buildings may find it advantageous to use two extraction systems due to varying use requirements. Level loop constructions in schools and hospitals will usually require more frequent aggressive cleaning than the fine cut pile carpet in the bank president's office.

The carpet construction, colour, type of soil, and traffic classification all impact the carpet maintenance frequencies and extraction selection. For great looking healthy carpet, plan your carpet maintenance programme, use the frequency schedule for guidelines, then work your plan.

Deep Cleaning

Prior to application of any cleaning agent, as much loose soil as possible should be removed. Pile lift the carpet by making one pass in the direction of the pile lay. Then pull the pile lifter backwards so the pile will be lifted and open. This will enhance penetration of the cleaning agent into the pile. If a pile lifter is not available, vacuum the carpet thoroughly. If the area to be cleaned is heavily soiled with any oily or greasy substance, then spray a fine mist of preconditioner over the area five to ten minutes prior to extraction cleaning. The following list shows the most common methods now in use for overall deep cleaning of carpet:

— Absorbent Compound Extraction

— Hot Water Extraction

Cleaning carpet with harsh alkaline detergents can be risky. In some cases, dyes might fade. Before using any detergent solution, always pretest on a carpet scrap or in an inconspicuous section of carpet to be sure it will not affect the colour. Allow the test area to completely dry before proceeding. If there is any colour change, stop. Continue to pretest until a safe product is found or call a carpet cleaning professional. The ideal carpet cleaning detergent solution will have the following characteristics:

— Is environmentally safe
— Has very low total volatile organic emissions that dissipate quickly
— Is anionic, nonionic, or combinations thereof.
— Has a pH of 9 or less
— Can be used at less than 150°F
— Has excellent cleaning ability
— Turns to a crisp powder when dry
— Will not dull the carpet
— Will not cause rapid resoil
— Will not attack dyes
— Will not be toxic
— Will not create static electricity
— Contains no optical brighteners

8

Menu Planning

Menu planning is the process of planning and scheduling intake of meals for a general or specific individual requirements. Beginning with menu planning, each control point plays a crucial role in determining the success or failure of a food and beverage operation. Each control point is a miniature system with its own structure and functions. Each basic operating activity has specific objectives, guidelines, standards, and internal processes that contribute to the success of the operation and the ultimate goal: guest satisfaction.

The process of planning a menu never ends; the final menu is never achieved. Rather, the process is ongoing, dynamic, and based on the expectations of the operation's present and potential guests—its target markets. From creating an image to communicating a plan for satisfying the guests, influencing the guests' purchase decisions, merchandising the correct products, and more, the menu has a continuous impact on all aspects of an operation.

A properly planned and well-designed menu stimulates revenue and increases the guest check average, because whenever a menu is presented to a guest, a sales transaction begins. And the menu not only creates but also reflects the operation's image. The image may be elegant, businesslike, fun, ethnic, or trendy, depending on what the target market(s) desire. The menu has an impact on every aspect of a food and beverage manager's job as well as the operation itself.

PLANNING PROCESS

The menu is not only an important control tool, it is also a sales, advertising, merchandising, and marketing tool. In this respect, the menu addresses both control and marketing—related concerns and blends them into a workable system. Because it lists the items an operation is offering for sale, a menu, in effect, communicates a property's food and beverage marketing plans. In developing its marketing plans, a property needs to assess the products, service, ambience (theme and atmosphere), and perceived value that its target market(s) expect. Items selected for inclusion in the menu should be based on the needs and desires of the operation's target markets.

In carrying out its marketing plans, the food and beverage operation must strive to meet or exceed the expectations of its target markets. Management must never forget the marketing implications of the menu planning process. Notice that the most important and numerous concerns involve the guest and the quality of menu items. These are also the most complex concerns. Others include cost, availability, and production/ operation concerns. In addition, menu planners should study the competition and the types of menu items offered by both direct and indirect competitors in the area.

It is especially necessary to consider items offered by competitors who are trying to attract the same target market(s). What are guests of other properties purchasing? Why? What are the selling prices? What can be done to make the property's own products and services special—and more attractive to guests? These and related questions with marketing implications constitute a primary source of information for menu planners in all types of food and beverage operations.

The complexity of menu planning in commercial properties depends upon the ambience of the food and beverage operation. Menu planning for table service restaurants is different from menu planning for banquet or buffet service operations. Ambience, the guests check average, and marketing concerns are prime examples of these differences. Many food and beverage operations have a specific theme and atmosphere.

French, Italian, and Chinese restaurants are examples of operations with ethnic themes. Others feature the cuisine of the American Southwest (for example, chilirelenos, tortillas, enchiladas) or Cajun cuisine (for example, jambalaya, gumbo, blackened redfish). Still others create a healthy ambience by capitalising on an atmosphere and theme built on open, airy, plant—filled facilities that serve high quality, light, fresh foods. In any case, menu items offered must be compatible with the theme and atmosphere of the operation.

In the past, food service managers often attempted to diversify their menus by adding many new menu items. Since most items were made from scratch, the number and variety of raw ingredients increased correspondingly. Another strategy, called "rationalisation," limits the menu to those items that best enhance the operation's image. Its objective is simplification for the sake of operational efficiency. An operation can offer several menu items that use the same raw ingredients. This cross-utilisation enables an operation to prepare and serve many menu selections with a limited number of raw ingredients.

When the menu is carefully planned to ensure a balance of menu selections in each category, the results of these new strategies can be a streamlining of the purchasing, receiving, storing, issuing, production, and serving control points. Today, as in the past, food service managers are searching for new menu item alternatives. The increasing number of high quality convenience foods has made it easier to offer new items without having to buy additional raw ingredients or elaborate equipment.

High-quality convenience products can be purchased in semi-prepared or fully prepared forms. Because they have built—in labour, they also reduce in-house labour requirements. Of course, convenience food products usually have a higher AP (as purchased) price than the raw ingredients from which they are made. It is always best to base initial menu plans on the needs and desires of the target market(s). However, several other factors may influence the menu selection. Among these factors are the recommended storage conditions (time and temperature); personnel skill levels; the product's availability and seasonality; the stability of quality and price levels; and the operation's ability to purchase, produce, and serve the menu items in a safe, sanitary, and cost-effective way.

Entrees are typically selected first in the menu planning process. It is important to consider not only the types of entrees, but also their costs, preparation methods, and compatibility with theme and atmosphere. A basic decision in planning the entree base concerns the number of entrees to offer. How many menu items should the operation provide? Some managers feel they should have something for everyone and, therefore, provide a wide range of entrees. This approach creates a number of problems that require careful planning and control to resolve.

The variety of entrees also affects the types and quantities of ingredients (each with its own standard purchase specifications) that must be received, stored, issued, produced, and served. A corresponding amount of preparation equipment and number of skilled personnel must also be available, and production/ service problems are more likely to occur. In summary, control is more complex. The reverse approach of making available only a limited number of entrees reduces these types of problems considerably. In the United States there are many specialty/theme restaurants that offer relatively few entrees.

By focusing on a specific segment of the market, this type of operation not only simplifies marketing techniques, but also minimises many in house production, serving and control problems. After selecting entrees, menu planners must choose menu items to complement the entrees. A common procedure is to plan appetisers and/or soups, followed by high—starch items and/or vegetables (if not part of the entree), then accompanying salads, and, finally, other menu components such as breads, desserts, and beverages. Trends in entree consumption affect the other items added to the menu.

Dining Trends

One dining trend compatible with many lifestyles is "grazing." Grazers are unlikely to select a full meal, but rather choose appetizers, salads, and desserts to complete their menu selections. Grazers are more likely to choose smaller portions of more menu items than to select a larger portion single entree. Therefore, menus featuring a wide selection of appetisers, salads, and desserts are popular with grazers. Menus are being designed with interchangeable courses, sometimes referred to as "modular cuisine."

The grazing trend is expected to continue and grow as guests change their eating habits and focus on the perceived high value of making multiple menu selections to "build their own" meals. The grazing trend seems to be particularly popular with the health and fitness-conscious baby boomers, whose lifestyles reflect their desire for variety. If a food and beverage operation's business is transient and the clientele changes frequently, the menu may be static (remain the same).

Generally, menus that change—dynamic menus—are preferable to static menus. However, menu variability depends on the seasonal availability of raw ingredients at reasonable costs, the number and types of courses offered, the potential for using leftovers and local ingredients, the preferences of the guests, the operation's image, and the desires of the target markets. When the business is highly repetitive and involves regular guests such as business people and others who reside in the local area, there is a greater need for daily specials that regularly change.

Often, daily specials feature local or regional fresh ingredients and permit the menu planner to take advantage of reduced costs and increased availability to add interest to a menu. A trend today in daily specials is to announce their availability on attractive, eye-catching iridescent or colourfully lighted menu boards and suggestively merchandise them to guests.

Menu Designing

The design of the menu can influence the guest's purchase decisions, stimulate sales of additional or preferable menu items, and increase the guest check average. Guests are influenced by visual cues provided by the menu. Readability, artwork, type styles, physical design, and layout play an important role in merchandising the food and beverage products that are profitable to the operation and satisfying to the guests. Menu items featured in these positions often draw the reader's attention because of their location. Of course, other devices such as art, pictures, and graphics can be used to draw the reader's attention elsewhere.

Menu Changes

Because conditions change, a food service operation's menu must also change. Menu changes are influenced by both external and internal factors.

External factors include consumer demands, economic conditions, the competition, supply levels, and industry trends. Consumer demands are perhaps the most important factor to consider in changing a menu. Management should first decide which potential markets it wants to attract with the modified menu. Then the proposed menu change must be evaluated in light of the negative and positive effects it may have on current guests. Economic conditions include the cost of ingredients and the potential profitability of new menu items.

Menu items offered by the competition may dictate choices to be made available. For example, a hotel food service located next to a restaurant offering the "best Chinese food in town" may elect not to serve Chinese cuisine. Supply levels relate the price to the quality and quantity of the proposed menu items. Supply levels are highly variable for some seasonal raw ingredients such as fresh fruits and vegetables. Industry trends provide general information about how the industry is responding to new demands. At present, an overall trend in many areas relates to a more sophisticated guest who is searching for an increasingly higher price-value relationship and who will pay more to receive more.

Internal factors that may result in a proposed menu change include the facility's meal pattern, concept and theme, operational system, and menu mix. The typical meal pattern is breakfast, lunch, and dinner. Management must decide if existing meal periods should be continued or altered. Expectations of guests have a direct influence on this decision. Any change must fit with the establishment's concept and theme.

A restaurant that is known as the best steakhouse in the city may do itself a disservice by adding an extensive variety of fresh fish and shellfish to the menu. An establishment's image may also rule out certain foods that do not blend with its theme and decor. For example, even though ethnic foods are growing in popularity, a hotel restaurant may find it difficult to fit ethnic foods into its projected image. Menu changes are also modified by the establishment's operational system. For example, if extensive new equipment purchases are crucial to the successful production and service of the menu item, the change may be too costly.

Also, the change may raise both food and labour costs to unacceptable levels. Or, in some cases, the skill levels of production and service personnel may not be adequate to successfully produce and present the new menu item. The operation's existing menu has a certain overall combination or mix of items. This menu mix will be affected by any change in individual items. All of these factors should be evaluated before menu changes are finalised and implemented.

PRICING METHODS

Commercial food service operations, as well as many institutional facilities, must establish appropriate selling prices for menu items. Objective pricing methods ensure that the property's profit requirements, as well as the value guests attach to the entire dining experience (including service, cleanliness, and ambience), are incorporated into the selling price. Pricing approaches are:

Subjective Methods

Although prices determine to a large extent whether financial goals of the operation are met, many managers use very subjective pricing methods. These methods establish prices, but generally fail to relate them to profit requirements or even costs. When the subject of pricing methods comes up, many managers speak about the art of pricing and suggest that intuition and special knowledge about guests' ability to pay are the most important considerations. Consider the following pricing methods and notice that each is based simply upon the manager's assumptions or guesses about what prices should be.

Reasonable Price Method: This method uses a price that the food service manager thinks will represent a value to the guest. The manager presumes to know—from the guest's perspective—what charge is fair and equitable. In other words, the manager asks, "If I were a guest, what price would I pay for the item being served?" The manager's best guess in answering this question becomes the product's selling price.

Highest Price Method: Using this plan, a manager sets the highest price that he or she thinks guests are willing to pay. The concept of value is stretched to the maximum and is then "backed off" to provide a margin of error in the manager's estimate.

Loss Leader Method: With this plan, an unusually low price is set for an item (or items). The manager assumes that guests will be attracted to the property to purchase the low priced items and that they will then select other items while they are there. Beverage or food prices on some items are set low to bring guests into the property, but purchases of other items are necessary for the operation to meet profit requirements. This pricing method is sometimes used as an "early bird" or senior citizen discount to attract specific segments of the market.

Intuitive Price Method: When prices are set by intuition alone, the manager takes little more than a wild guess about the selling price. Closely related to this approach is a trial-and-error pricing plan-if one price doesn't work, another is tested. The intuitive price method differs from the reasonable price method in that there is less effort to determine what represents value from the guests' perspective.

These pricing methods are based on assumptions, hunches, and guesses. Such methods are generally ineffective because they do not consider profit requirements and the product costs necessary to put the item on the table. These subjective pricing methods may be common in the food service industry simply because they have been used in the past, because the manager setting prices has no information about product costs or profit requirements to work with, and/or because the manager is not familiar with more objective methods. In today's market, with increased consumer demands for value in dining, and with higher purchase prices for products needed by the property, these plans seldom work.

Multiplier Methods

Some pricing methods use a mark-up by a multiplier based upon food costs for menu items. The methods are designed to cover all costs and to yield the desired profit. The following sections examine ingredients mark-up pricing, prime—ingredient mark-up pricing, and mark-up with accompaniment costs. Advantages and disadvantages of these methods are also discussed.

Ingredients Mark-Up Method: The ingredients mark-up pricing method attempts to consider all product costs: food costs when pricing food items, and beverage costs when pricing beverages.

A base selling price is not necessarily the final selling price. The simple output from formulas may not be an appropriate final selling price. Rather, a base selling price is considered a starting point from which other factors must be assessed and the price adjusted accordingly. The multiplier determined in step 2 is generally based on the desired food (or beverage) cost percentage (which might be established by in-house assessment procedures or from budget development).

Prime-Ingredient Mark-Up Method: The prime-ingredient mark-up pricing method differs from the ingredients mark-up method in that only the cost of the prime ingredient is marked up. In addition, the multiplier used must be greater than the multiplier used when considering the total cost of all ingredients. The prime-ingredient approach assumes that the costs of all ingredients change in proportion to the prime ingredient. That is, when the prime ingredient's cost increases 10 percent, then other ingredients' costs are assumed to increase also by 10 percent.

Mark-Up with Accompaniment Costs: Using the mark-up with accompaniment costs pricing method, managers determine ingredient costs based only upon entree items and then add a standard accompaniment or "plate" cost to this amount before multiplying by a multiplier. This plate cost is an average cost for all non-entree and other relatively inexpensive items including salad, vegetables, bread, butter, and non-alcoholic beverages. A disadvantage may be that plate costs are not truly representative of food costs associated with these other items. Also, managers must establish a reasonable and objective multiplier that relates to profit requirements. If this is not done, the mark-up with accompaniment costs pricing method is no better than the subjective pricing methods discussed earlier.

Determining the Multiplier: The mark-up pricing methods just discussed are simple to use and, for that reason, are commonly used in the food service industry. A significant disadvantage, however, involves determining the multiplier. How does a manager decide this? For many managers, it is a subjective decision based primarily upon experience and "rule of thumb" (such as the traditional 40 percent food cost). Should managers use last year's average food cost percentage? Should they use a statistic supplied by a national, state, or other food service association or consulting firm?

It is, of course, possible to use a multiplier based upon the planned food and other costs from the operating budget. If, on the average, menu items are priced to yield the food cost percentage dictated by the budget, planners have developed a simple foundation for generating revenue sufficient to cover food costs and to yield a contribution margin (food revenue minus food costs) sufficient for other expenses and profit requirements. The little time required to generate and use this multiplier based on the operating budget may make it especially cost effective for many small-volume operations. However, the impact of sales mix cannot be overlooked.

If, for example, increased unit sales of a higher food cost percentage item replace sales of its counter parts with lower food cost percentages, the average food cost percentage can be made according to budget-but with undesirable financial results. There are other potential disadvantages of using simple multiplier pricing methods. For example, these pricing methods do not reflect higher or lower labour, energy, or other costs associated with production of specific menu items.

Rather, they either assume that all operating costs relate in some direct way to food costs or that these cost differences can be ignored. These assumptions may not be warranted as one considers the extensive amount of labour required to prepare some items relative to others. The mark-up pricing methods using a multiplier also assume that all food costs associated with producing a menu item are known. In fact, many other costs may be excluded from the cost of ingredients used as the base for the multiplier.

Contribution Margin Method

The term contribution margin refers to the amount left after a menu item's food cost is subtracted from its selling price. The contribution margin is the amount that the sale of a menu item contributes to pay for all non-food costs allocated to the food service operation and to help with profit requirements. With a contribution margin pricing method, managers can set base selling prices for menu items by following two steps:

— Determine the average contribution margin required per guest by dividing all non-food costs plus required profit by the number of expected guests.

— Determine the base-selling price for a menu item by adding the average contribution margin required per guest to the item's standard food cost.

Advantages of this method are its ease and practicality when reasonably accurate information is available from the operating budget. It is also useful in those operations where costs associated with serving each guest are basically the same, with the exception of varying food costs. Also, this method tends to reduce the range of selling prices on the menu, since the only difference is reflected in the actual food cost incorporated into the selling price. A potential disadvantage of this method is that it assumes that each guest should pay the same share of the property's non-food costs and profit requirements.

Ratio Method

The ratio pricing method determines the relationship between food costs and all on-food costs plus profit requirements and uses this ratio to develop base selling prices for menu items. The three steps to ratio pricing are as follows:

— Determine the ratio of food costs to all non-food costs plus required profit by dividing all non-food costs plus profit by food costs.

— Calculate the amount of non-food costs plus profit required for a menu item by multiplying the standard food cost of the menu item by the ratio calculated in step 1.

— Determine the base selling price of a menu item by adding the result of step 2 to the standard food cost of the menu item.

The ratio method of menu pricing is simple to use and can be based on operating budget requirements. However, it does have several disadvantages. In an operation offering both food and beverages, it is necessary to separate non-food costs and profit requirements between the two revenue centres. Also, under this pricing method, each meal assumes an equal share of non-food costs and profit. The ratio pricing method does not compensate for higher labour costs associated with the preparation of labourintensive menu items.

Prime Costs Method

The term prime costs refers to the most significant costs in a food service operation: product (food and beverage) and labour. A simple prime costs pricing method involves assessing the labour costs for the food service operation and .factoring these costs into the pricing equation. The three steps to simple prime costs pricing are as follows:

— Determine the labour cost per guest by dividing labour costs by the number of expected guests.

— Determine the prime costs per guest by adding the labour cost per guest to the menu item's food cost.

— Determine the menu item's base selling price by dividing the prime costs per guest by the desired prime costs percentage.

The food cost for the menu item is the standard cost derived by costing the item's standard recipe. Labour costs and estimated .guests are obtained from the approved operating budget. The desired prime costs percentage combines projected food and labour cost percentages, also from the operating budget. The food service manager would then adjust this base selling price in relation to other factors, such as the operation's target markets and the competition. Advantages of this method are its focus on both food and labour costs and the fact that it is easy to use. An obvious disadvantage is the need to assign an equal labour cost to each menu item, even though the actual labour costs for menu items may vary greatly.

With the specific prime costs pricing method the food service manager develops multipliers for menu items so that the base selling prices for the items cover their food costs and their fair share of labour costs. Items with extensive preparation have higher labour costs and should have higher mark-ups. Conversely, items not requiring extensive preparation have lower labour costs that can be reflected in a lower mark-up. The manager first divides all menu items into two categories: those that do and those that do not involve extensive preparation labour. The definition of extensive preparation labour is left to the manager to determine.

Pricing Considerations

The result of menu pricing calculations is a base selling price. This is because the simple output of formulas used in the examples may not be an appropriate final selling price for a menu item. Rather, it is a starting point from which other factors must be assessed. The concept of value (price relative to quality) is always important. Guests pay for more than just the product (food and beverage) when they visit the operation. Quality of service, cleanliness of the facility, and atmosphere are also part of the dining experience and should, even if subjectively, be factored into the selling price decision.

The basic law of supply and demand is another factor to be considered. Ultimately, the price that can be charged is established by the guests themselves as they decide whether to return to the property. Volume concerns must also be considered. As fewer guests are served, overhead charges per guest increase; selling prices must be higher. The reverse is also true: more guests may allow the manager to reduce overhead costs in the pricing decision.

The price charged by the competition for a similar product is another concern. The more an operation can differentiate its products from those of the competition, the more freedom the operation has in setting a selling price. For example, perhaps two properties offer a similar steak dinner. While the price charged for the steak is important, there are other factors that may influence people to visit one property or the other.

Perhaps one property provides entertainment, while the other offers an attractive atmosphere. Emphasising the differences between the property's own products and services and those offered by other businesses is one way to remain competitive. One technique that can be used to attract guests from competitors is lowering menu prices. This may succeed in bringing more people into an operation, but only if the lower priced items are considered by guests as substitutes for what the competition offers.

If there are no significant differences between what one operation offers and what the competition offers, then guests may see price as the determining factor in selecting one property over the others. However, if there are non-price-related differences that are important to guests (such as atmosphere, entertainment, etc.) this technique may not work. Raising prices is also a way of responding to pressures from the competition. With higher prices, fewer menu items will need to be sold for the operation to meet profit requirements.

However, raising a menu item's selling price may be effective only if the increased revenue from the price increase makes up for the revenue lost as demand falls off and current guests begin to buy other menu items as substitutes. In fact, in some cases, a more effective strategy for increasing total revenue may be lowering a menu item's selling price. Lowering prices may increase the volume of unit sales, and this increase may produce an increase in total revenue. What we are really talking about here is the concept of elasticity of demand.

Elasticity is a term economists use to describe how the quantity demanded responds to changes in price. If a certain percentage price change creates a larger percentage change in the quantity demanded, the demand is elastic and the item is considered to be price-sensitive.

Menu Evaluation

The menu is a most important tool influencing the success or failure of food and beverage operation. But how should menus be evaluated to determine whether the most profitable menu items are being sold? The process of menu engineering is an increasingly popular approach to this problem of menu evaluation. There are two measures of how good a menu item is: its popularity and its profitability. A popular menu item is ordered frequently by guests. A profitable menu item generates a high contribution margin. Menu items can be evaluated in terms of both their popularity and profitability.

To classify each menu item into one of the four basic categories, managers must develop a practical way to define and measure the relative profitability and popularity of each menu item. This can be accomplished by using information about standard food costs and frequency of unit sales. The basis of a menu item's profitability is not the level of its food cost, but its contribution margin. Some managers assume that the lower a menu item's food cost percentage, the more profitable the sale of the item is to the operation. In other words, the lower the percentage of revenue needed to pay for the food needed for the menu item, the larger the percentage of revenue available for all other expenses and profit.

While this theory sounds good, it can be easily disproved. Information about frequency of unit sales for each menu item can be gathered by tallying the number of each item sold during some specified time period (such as two weeks). This information can be abstracted from guest checks or, more frequently, by analysis of unit sales information from the electronic register or production records indicating leftovers, if applicable. Popular items are those with a relatively high menu mix percentage.

Accordingly, "star" menu items are those with relatively high contribution margins and high menu mix percentages, while items classified as "dogs" score relatively low on both measures. In performing a menu engineering analysis, it is not enough to consider menu items individually. Each item's contribution margin and menu mix percentage will provide measures for the item's levels of profitability and popularity, but the problem is to evaluate how high or low these levels are in comparison with all other menu items.

Menu Engineering

The benefits of menu engineering can only accrue if

information gained from the menu engineering analysis is used to improve the menu. What can a food and beverage manager do with this knowledge about the various food item classifications?

Plowhorses Management

First, let's consider plowhorses. Guests like these items, but, unfortunately, plowhorses do not contribute their fair share of contribution margin. Possible strategies for managing a plowhorse menu item include:

— *Increase prices carefully*: Perhaps the item is popular because it represents a great value to guests. If prices could be increased, the item may still represent a good value, may remain popular, and may generate a higher contribution margin. This alternative may be most effective when the item is unique to the property and cannot be obtained elsewhere.

— *Test for demand*: If there is no strong resistance to price increases, it may be useful to complement an increased price with other strategies such as repackaging the item or repositioning it on the menu. These other strategies may be designed to maintain or increase the item's popularity while generating a higher contribution margin through the increase in selling price. If prices are to be increased, this should probably be done in several stages rather than all at once.

— *Relocate the item to a lower profile on the menu*: Depending upon the menu layout, certain areas of a menu represent a better location than others. A plowhorse can be relocated to a less desirable area of the menu. Since the item is popular, some guests will search it out. Others will be drawn to higher profile areas of the menu that list more profitable items the property wishes to sell.

— *Shift demand to more desirable items*: Menu engineering allows the manager to determine which items to sell-those high in popularity and high in contribution margin.
— *Combine with lower cost products*: The contribution margin of a plowhorse can be increased if lower cost meal accompaniments are offered with the entree. Perhaps, for example, higher priced vegetables and dessert accompaniments can be replaced with other, less expensive items without reducing the item's popularity. If this can be done, the contribution margin will increase.
— *Assess the direct labour factor*: The food and beverage manager should know if there is a significant amount of direct labour required to produce the plowhorse item. If an item with a low contribution margin does not have a significant amount of direct labour involved in production, the manager may be able to justify the lower contribution margin since fewer revenue dollars will be required to compensate for labour cost.
— *Consider portion reduction*: If the portion size is reduced, the product cost will be decreased and the contribution margin will increase. This alternative must be viewed with caution, of course, since the guest's perception of value may decrease when the portion size is reduced.

Puzzle Management

Puzzles are items that are high in: contribution margin but low in popularity—items the food and beverage manager desires to sell since their contribution margins relatively high. The challenge is to find ways to increase the number of guests ordering these items. Alternatives include:

Shift demand to these items: Techniques include repositioning the items to more visible areas of the menu, renaming them, using suggestive selling techniques, developing advertising campaigns, using table tents, using buttons and badges on server uniforms, highlighting items on menu boards at the entrance to the dining area, and other strategies to increase the item's popularity.

Consider a price decrease: Perhaps an item is low in popularity because it does not represent a value to guests. If this is the case, the selling price might be decreased with the contribution margin still remaining higher than average. This could lead to increased popularity, since a reduced selling price would represent a greater value to the guest.

Add value to the item: Offering a larger portion size, adding more expensive meal accompaniments or garnishes, and using higher quality ingredients are among the ways that value can be increased. These techniques may lead to increased popularity and to a contribution margin that is lower, but still higher than the average generated by the menu.

Managing Stars

Stars are items that are high in contribution margin and high in popularity. The best advice for managing stars includes:

— *Maintain rigid specifications*: Do not attempt to alter the quality of the product being served.

— *Place in a highly visible location on the menu*: Stars are items that the food and beverage operator wants to sell. Therefore, make sure guests are aware of their availability.

— *Test for selling price inelasticity*: Perhaps the star is popular because it is a significant value to the guest.

Or, perhaps the star is not available in its existing form elsewhere in the, marketplace. These might be two instances in which the price could be increased without a decrease in popularity.

— *Use suggestive selling techniques*: Some of the techniques for shifting demand to puzzles might also be useful for stars.

Managing Dogs

Dogs (items that are low in contribution margin €lnd low in popularity) are obvious candidates for removal from the menu. After all, they do not contribute their fair share of contribution margin and they are not popular. Alternatively, the selling price could be increased, since this would at least generate a higher contribution margin. When all dog requires a significant amount of direct labour, does not permit sufficient use of leftovers, and has a relatively short storage life, the reasons for removing the item from the menu become more compelling.

To this point, how a menu item classification system lends itself to the development of improved menus by more effective management of individual menu items. Are there other advantages to the use of the menu engineering process? Yes, it can be used to evaluate the worth of the entire menu. Consider, for example, the current practice in the industry when a menu is revised. The manager, guests, employees, and others may offer their opinions about the revisions. They may subjectively assess the menu's "worth" and offer their views about its improvements over earlier versions.

9

TABLE SERVICE

In today's society, which continues to move toward more computers and impersonal service, the customer wants smiles and human interaction in place of cold, nonthinking, unemotional computers. It becomes essential that the restaurant and banquet managers of the twenty-first century know how to give and train their employees to provide excellent service to their guests. Too many times, the service person is blamed for good or poor service. It appears to the guest that the service person should take the credit or blame. However, the blame or credit falls on the manager It is up to the manager to set the tone of the business.

If the manager cares about his guests, then the message will be loud and clear to the service staff. If the manager gives the impression that he is only there because he has to be and that the guests are an imposition on his time, the service staff will get that message also. Over and over again, the one common thread in all restaurants that are judged to be outstanding is the care and concern of the owner or manager toward the guests and staff.

Service should be the foundation on which restaurants are built. Service is not allowing one customer to light his own cigarette, service is water glasses full, service is treating your customers as they should be, like honoured guests. And it's not second nature. It must be taught. Kevin O'Donnell, the Inn Manager at the Inn at Shelburne Farms in Shelburne, Vermont, states that guests are experts concerning the cost of food. He asks his staff, "Why should someone pay ten times more in a restaurant for a Chicken Kiev than buying it already prepared at a gourmet section in a supermarket and eating it at their kitchen table?" The answer is the service that is provided to our guests.

In a restaurant, the manager should be walking around talking to the guests. In a banquet, and fingers naturally go. The water and wine glasses are always filled. It is never necessary to ask for the ketchup or butter or more bread. A second cup of tea or coffee is poured before the guests request it. The correctly added check is even presented to the guests without having to be requested; and the service person and host thank the guest for patronising the restaurant. It bears repeating: Excellent service is friendliness combined with competency. One of the points is to have "fast and efficient service." The most important ingredient in successful service is the human element, that is, concern for the guest. For example, Walt Disney World has been praised for its excellent service, and it has been featured in the book and the television show, In Search of Excellence.

According to Tony Jenkins, all new employees have to attend orientation classes, where they learn about the history, philosophy, and style of Disney. All service staff employees receive an initial three-day training period with approved trainers. These trainers are employees who have worked at the restaurant for a period of time and who are themselves products of the Disney training classes. On the first day at the job, the new employees follow and observe their trainers for half a day. This procedure is called shadowing. During this time, the trainers explain how to present the menu and how to serve the food. All of the methods are standard for all service staff at Disney.

In the second half of the day, the new employees carry out the trays for the trainers. The trainers, since they are regular service persons, have their own stations in the restaurant. All the training in this phase is accomplished on the job, and the new employees have to meet and follow all the standards set down by Disney. For example, every item that comes from the kitchen to the dining room must be carried on a tray. Disney insists on the same standards for all its restaurants, the same service to all its guests at all locations. On the second day of training, the new employees have contact with the guests. They approach the guests, present the menu, and take the order. The trainers are now shadowing the new employees.

Throughout the day, the new employees are encouraged, reminded, and taught the correct ways to serve Disney guests. On the third day, each new employee begins the day by being assigned two or three of the trainer's tables. By the end of the day, the new employee is waiting on and serving all five tables in the station. "The key to the Disney training is follow-up," says Tony Jenkins. "Each restaurant has periodic service meetings. Perhaps one or two a month to go over new procedures, price changes, and new menu items." Another key is the use of mystery shoppers at Disney. These shoppers patronise the restaurants for the sole purpose of observing their operation. Included in their observations is a report on the service by the service person. Therefore, the management of the restaurant has an unbiased report on its operation and can take steps to clear up any problems.

Ineffective Service

Ineffective service can be frustrating and embarrassing for a restaurant. For instance, you, as a guest, are served your meal, and a few minutes later your dining companion is served. Or, how many times have you had to wait for a check before you could get to that show on time? Guests tend to remember their last experience in a restaurant. He further states that a lack of friendly service rates as a leading cause for poor sales. Guests often try five different restaurants before encountering some sort of satisfactory experience. Statistics indicate that 93 percent of restaurant failures stem from poor management. People who manage restaurants very often have no concept of how to please their guests.

Many managers prefer operational tasks to the actual running of a restaurant. Employees, during the first thirty days after being hired, will establish their work pattern, often based on their manager's style. If a manager fails to conduct formal training sessions and fails to express the restaurant's philosophy on guest service, the results will be poor service from the employees. After all, the manager does not seem to care about the guests. On the other hand, if you have a manager who cares and trains the staff properly, the business will prosper.

The intention was and is to develop a great front of the house so that people will feel good while they are eating in the restaurant. In a sense, the core is honesty in hosting, while providing really great, high quality, interesting food and wine in a non-threatening atmosphere. Every person who considers a career in the restaurant field must realise that most guests do not come to a restaurant or banquet facility merely to eat. In the field of psychology there is a well-known theory formulated by A. H. Maslow called Maslow's Hierarchy. This hierarchy deals with human needs. Maslow cites five basic needs that an average person possesses.

These are the physiological need and the needs for safety, love and belonging, esteem, and self-actualisation. The first four are referred to as dependent needs because they are obtained from other people. Self-actualisation comes from oneself. Restaurant managers should know and understand how these needs affect their guests. The theory states that a person must significantly satisfy one need before moving on to the next need. However, it has been demonstrated that it is possible to satisfy portions of two needs simultaneously. Let us relate Maslow's Hierarchy to the restaurant business and understand why this theory is important to a restaurant and banquet manager. A restaurant and/or banquet manager should realise that two of the needs, the physiological and the need for love, most often will have been met before the guest enters the hospitality establishment. The final need, self-actualisation, is an internal need that the manager deals with indirectly.

The major needs that the manager and the employees must deal with are those for safety and esteem. The physiological need means that if we do not have enough money to provide food for ourselves or our family, we will spend the greatest portion of our time trying to earn enough money or to obtain food to satisfy this need. All restaurant guests have satisfied this need because they are not starving. Once the physiological need is satisfied, the person moves on to the next need-the safety need. The safety need can play an important part in the success or failure of a restaurant or banquet facility.

PRINCIPLES OF TABLE SERVICE

Competency

The manager must teach and reinforce correct serving methods to the service staff so that these methods become second nature. The Random House Dictionary defines competent as "having suitable skill, experience, etc., for some purpose." Competent service in a restaurant has one main purpose: the guest will leave the establishment pleased with the dining experience. Competency in a restaurant can best be described in the following way: Competency occurs when the customers do not have to ask the service person for any item during a meal. The water glasses are refilled. The meals are served without the service persons asking which guest receives which menu item.

In short, the guests know they have had a great dining experience because the service person brought all items to them before they could think of asking for it. Great restaurants instill competency in their service staff through great attention to details, training, and follow-up. The success of a restaurant depends on the manager. If the manager overlooks the little details, the service staff will also overlook the little details. However, if the manager pays attention to details, the service staff will consistently follow the manager's lead.

Competency comes from management. Management must teach their staff the proper way to serve their guests. In addition, management continuously monitors their service. The staff must be reminded about what they are doing correctly and incorrectly. Many people, including restaurant reviewers, restaurant owners, and guests, have stated that excellent service can compensate for average food; but great food cannot compensate for bad service. Excellent service is the result of the two factors, competency and friendliness.

Competency is serving food and drinks to the guest in the correct manner. Friendliness is a characteristic that the dining room and/or banquet manager must encourage in service staff. At times, the manager has to be concerned if the service staff become too friendly with the guests. This friendliness leads to informality and then sloppiness. Friendliness, if done correctly, is an extremely important aspect of excellent service. However, the service staff must also be competent in order to provide excellent service. Anything being done incorrectly must be corrected immediately. Managers are taught to be coaches, and to coach cast members in the correct way to serve. The key to competent service is training.

Sidetowel

The sidetowel has two purposes. First, it can be used as an insulator; the service person can pick up and serve dinners with the sidetowel rather than risking getting burned from handling hot plates. Second, if there is any type of spill, the service person has a cloth to clean up the spill. There is no need to waste valuable time running back to the kitchen to obtain cloths to clean up the mess. Therefore, the sidetowel becomes a time-saver. When the sidetowel is not used for any of the above purposes, it should be placed over the service person's left arm, not stuck in the back pocket like a handkerchief. It must always be clean. If the service person is not using the sidetowel as an insulator to serve food, then the sidetowel should be placed over the right arm.

Trays

A wonderful invention was made for waitpeople: the tray. Two basic types of trays are used in the restaurant industry. Large trays, called hotel ovals, are used to carry food and plates to and from the guest. The other type are small round, rectangular, or oval trays (called tea trays) which are generally used to serve drinks. Large trays enable the service person to carry many items at once, as opposed to delivering food as they do in diners and coffee shops, item by item. It may be impressive to see a service person carrying eight dinners stacked up on both arms. However, using a tray is much more professional looking, efficient, safe, and sanitary than using the style called arm service.

Many of the best establishments insist that waitpeople use a tray to carry all items. The server must use a tray even if it is to carry a water pitcher or one coffee cup. Waitpeople should not be allowed to serve guests directly from the tray without putting the tray on a traystand, as it creates a safety hazard. Dining room and banquet managers who insist that the service staff use trays will have a much more competent service staff than managers who do not. Once the service staff form the habit of using trays, it becomes second nature.

Soon their service improves, because they are carrying more items on each trip between the dining room and the kitchen. As a result, they make fewer trips and save themselves a most valuable commodity: time. Besides enabling servers to carry more food and beverages to tables, using a tray is safer and more sanitary than using arm service. The tray is bigger than a plate. Therefore, anyone walking past will most likely see the tray and avoid a possible accident. Using a tray is more sanitary because the plates do not slide down the server's arm into one another. When this happens, one guest's gravy ends up on the other guest's plate.

Using a tray is more eye-appealing and pleasing to the guest because the plates do not slide down the server's arm into one another. However, the greatest reason for using a tray is that all the food can be delivered to the guests' table at the same time. This makes the guests' meal more enjoyable, and the restaurant more efficient. Small trays are used to bring drinks from the bar or one or two items from the kitchen. Some establishments will allow their servers to serve the guest directly from the tray, but that may create a safety hazard. Other establishments, like Walt Disney World, insist that the servers place the tray on a sidestand and serve from the sidestand to the guest. Whatever the policies of the establishment, using a tray to serve food is much more efficient than using arm service.

Trays can be set down on a permanent table in the dining room called a side-board or service station. Or they can be placed on lightweight devices called traystands. Traystands are excellent for use in a restaurant or at banquets because they are light enough to be carried by the server in one hand, while carrying a tray of food in the other hand. Therefore, the service person can carry the stand right to the guest table. This saves the service person time and extra steps, because the tray is right next to the table instead of being located a distance from the table.

Traystands open easily and are secure, so they are easy to use and safe. Using trays and having traystands located near the guests' table is the most efficient way to deliver food to the guests. There is a correct way to lift and put down a tray on the traystand. First, when training the staff, they should be taught the parts of the tray-stand. Make certain that they know all the parts and how they operate. There are two legs which open up and have cloth supports which hold the traystand together. The service person's body must be lined up parallel with the cloth supports. If the waitpeople line up correctly, their hands will not get tangled with the metal supports when they put down or pick up the tray. Waitpeople should be taught to line their body up even with the traystand.

The opening of the traystand should be at a right angle with the server's body. In order to protect their clean shirts from the dirty tray, service persons should place a clean napkin or cloth on their shoulder. The tray should be in balance before reaching the shoulder. The tray is then slid onto the service person's shoulder. Most waitpeople pick up the tray with their left hand under the tray and slide it onto their left shoulder because they control the tray with their right hand. However, it does not matter which shoulder the tray is carried on as long as it is carried properly. The service person's hand should be placed under the tray. The larger tray or hotel oval is usually carried while it is resting and balanced on the palm of the server's hand.

Loading tray: Trays are designed with either a nonslip surface such as an abrasive material or without it. If the tray does not have a nonslip material, the staff should be taught to take a damp, clean cloth, and put it on the tray. Even if the tray is made with a nonslip material, a clean cloth placed on the tray will make the service look more professional. In loading a tray, the heaviest items should be placed on the side of the tray that will be closest to the server's body. This will allow the server's shoulder to bear the brunt of the weight and allow the server to have more control over the tray. When more experienced servers carry the tray by balancing it on their fingertips, they place the heaviest items in the center of the tray.

The lighter items and glasses are placed to the outside of the tray or away from the service person's shoulder. Items with spouts and handles should have their spouts and handles facing the center of the tray. When serving food, the servers should be instructed to keep all hot items together. If it is necessary to carry both hot and cold food on the same tray, instruct their servers to separate the cold food from the hot food. Plates should never be stacked on top of each other unless plate covers are used. When serving soup, the cups should be placed around a stack of saucers. The soup should not be placed on the saucers until the server places the tray on the traystand.

When removing dirty dishes, the establishment should have an organised system for loading trays so that all plates are stacked neatly. This means all bread and butter plates are stacked on each other, instead of having a dinner plate on top of a bread and butter plate, with forks, knives, and spoons stuck in between them. It must be emphasised that the only way the staff will load their trays properly is if they are taught correctly by the manager. Once the training is complete, there must be consistent reinforcement by the manager; that is, correction and reinstruction if done incorrectly, and praise if done correctly.

The proper way to load a tray of dirty dishes. The silverware is separated from the plates. The top plate has all of the leftover food on it. When the server brings the food into the kitchen, it will be easy to unload the tray. The improper way to stack dirty dishes. The dishes are placed on the tray in no specific arrangement. Originally, they were thought of as rules, but they should be renamed guidelines because rules are too rigid for the dining room business. Perhaps that is why they were not and are not enforced consistently. Often, because of circumstances beyond the server's control, common sense must prevail when serving guests.

Ladies First

This means that if there is a party of two couples (two men and two women), the service person serves one woman and then the next woman. The service person serves in this order: woman #1, woman #2, man #1, man #2. If the server can easily determine who is the older woman at the table, she should be served first. There are instances when the server would break this guideline. Children should be served before adults. Then serve the women, then the men. People always wonder if this can be done. The server first took the order for drinks. She returned and served the youngest child his cola. Then she walked past the mother to serve the older son his soda. She returned to their mother to serve her drink. And finally, the father was served his drink. It did not take that long to serve all four guests. She served all drinks from the guests' right side with her right hand.

Throughout the meal, service was performed quickly and competently. The dining room was filled and the service was superb. It added to the great food and pleasant atmosphere of the restaurant. Another exception to this guideline is when serving a banquet, where the room is set up with long banquet tables seating more than ten people. With long banquet tables it makes little sense to skip over the men because there are so many guests at the table. If a server is working at a banquet where the banquet table has ten or more people on each side of the table, it is more logical to serve the guests in sequential order. The waiter is serving food properly to the guest. He is serving from the guest's left side with his left hand.

Serving Methods

There is a logical and practical reason for this guideline. If the service person served with the right hand from the left side of the guests it would create a potentially dangerous and awkward situation. The service person is putting his or her arm right in the faces of the guests. This could be most unappetising if the waiter has body odor. Also, the guests would have to back away in order to prevent the service person from brushing or hitting them with his arm. It is also dangerous for the service person. There are times when a guest does not pay attention to the service person and moves unexpectedly. When the service person sees the guest moving quickly, the server's arm can be swung out and away from the guest if the service is being done correctly. The chance of an accident is reduced by proper service. Because the service person is serving with the left hand, service should proceed in a clockwise direction.

Many people have trouble with the concept of clockwise and counterclockwise; a simple way to remember the correct direction is "to follow your nose." Proceed in the direction that your nose is pointing. Serve food from guest's left side with your left hand and follow your nose. There are a couple of exceptions to this guideline also. Serving food to guests seated at a booth or a table positioned against a wall requires a different set of procedures. The service person must serve and pick up with the same hand. When two guests are talking to each other, the service person does not interrupt their conversation by serving the food properly. Instead, he or she serves one guest from the left side, the other from the right side. When serving from the right side, the right hand should be used. If there is a physical item in the way (like a pole) or the table is positioned in such a way that makes it impossible to serve the guests from their left, they should be served from their right side.

Beverages serving

Because a large majority of people are right handed, the glasses and cups for beverages are put on the right side of the guest. It is logical that the service person would pour beverages from the right side of the guest. Therefore, to be consistent, all beverages are served from the right side. When serving an alcoholic beverage, a cocktail napkin should be placed in front of the guest. The beverage should then be placed on the cocktail napkin. If there is a meal in front of the guest, the service person will place the beverage above the spoons and knives on the right side of the guest.

When service persons have to pour water, wine, or coffee into a glass or cup already on the table they must not pick up the glass or cup, unless leaving the glass or cup on the table would create a safety hasard. The proper way to pour water is to pour with the right hand, keeping the left hand folded behind the back. Some establishments prefer that the service person hold the sidetowel (with the left hand) under the lip of the glass to catch any drips or spills. Water glasses should be filled three-quarters to the top of the glass.

Food brought to the table

One of the most annoying situations for a guest is to be served first and then have to wait for others at the table to be served their food. This creates two problems for the guests. Guests with proper manners will wait for the whole table to be served before they begin to eat their meal. Most likely their food will get cold, as the service person has to return to the kitchen to obtain the rest of the food. The manager should insist that all food reach the table at the same time. This is especially true at banquets when the guests have their choice of two main entrees. All guests must be served the meal at the same time even if half of them are eating chicken and the other half beef.

Do not remove any plates from the table unitl the end of meal

It is a mystery why wait-people remove plates from guests before all the guests at the table are finished eating their meal. This implies to the guests who have not finished their meal that they are taking too long to eat and must hurry and finish their meal. Of course, if a guest is done and pushes the plate to indicate he or she wants it to be cleared away, then take the plate away even if the others have not finished their meal. Another part of this guideline is that a new course must never be served until the dishes from the previous course have been removed from the table. This is another of the strict competency rules that are enforced at Walt Disney World: A server must remove the soup course before being allowed to serve the salad course. The only exception to this guideline may occur during a banquet, Because most banquets are on a strict time schedule, if the banquet manager waited for all guests to complete every course it could put the banquet behind schedule.

Dont scrape dirty plates on the table

This is the most irritating and unappetising habit a service person can have. Some waitpeople take the dirty dishes and stack them-one on top of another-right in front of the guests. Some of them will even dump the cigarette and cigar ashes from the dirty ashtray into the leftover mashed potatoes. If the restaurant or banquet establishment allows smoking, there is a proper way to change the ashtrays. The service person should bring to the table a clean ashtray. The clean ashtray should be turned upside down and placed over the dirty (capped ashtray). This acts as a cover, so as the service person removes the ashtrays, no ashes will spill onto the guests' table or into their food. The server places the capped ashtray behind his back and with his free hand places the clean ashtray (the cap) back on the table.

Clearing Dirty Dishes from the table

The guest's dirty dishes must be cleared with the service person's right hand, except when it makes more sense to clear from the left side (then it should be done with the service person's left hand illustrates how the waitress uses common sense by removing the bread and butter plate with her left hand from the guest's left side. She does so because if she removed the bread and butter plate from the guest's right side, she would have to reach in front of him.

Other Hints

Whichever hand you are using to serve or pick up, place that foot forward for balance. For example, if serving food with your left hand, place your left foot forward. If a guest places a dirty dish on his or her left side (to the left of the fork), the service person should remove the dish from the guest's left side with his left hand.

Keep in mind that the above are guidelines, not rules. The most important criteria are the comfort and safety of the guest. If you have to serve from "the wrong side" for the guest's comfort, do it.

1. Ladies are served before men
2. In French service, food is served from the guest's right side with the service person's right hand; in Russian service, food is served from the guest's left side with the platter in the service person's left hand, while serving with the right hand.
3. Beverages are served from the guest's right side with the service person's right hand.
4. All guests' food must be brought to the table at the same time.
5. Guest plates should not be removed from the table until all guests are finished eating their meals.
6. Dirty plates should never be stacked or scraped on the guest's table.
7. Dirty dishes are cleared from the guest's right side with the service person's right hand.

In French service, food is served from the guest's right side with the service person's right hand. In French a la carte service, the service person has to transfer food from a pan at the guerdon to plate. The plate is then served to the guest from the guest's right side with the waiter using his right hand. In Russian service, food is served from the guest's left side with the platter in the service person's left hand, while serving with the right hand.

This is the most confusing and contradictory of all the guidelines. In Russian service, clean plates are put down from the guest's right side with the service person's right hand. The food is then brought out on a silver platter. After the food has been presented to the guest, the service person transfers the food from the tray to the plate. This is accomplished by holding the tray in the left hand. The service person should serve the guest from the left side with the right hand. Even though this method will make the service person put an arm in front of the guest, making the guest back away, this is the method that has been taught since the beginning of Russian service.

The method probably originated because it is easier for the service person to transfer food from the platter to the plate. At times it can be difficult to manipulate the serving fork and spoon. There is a chance that the food may slip out of the fork and spoon. In order to be consistent with proper serving techniques, Russian service should be changed to have the service staff hold the tray in their right hands and serve the food with their left hands from the guest's right side. This would be safer and less awkward than the current system.

Styles of Service and Place Settings

Waiters learned how to serve guests properly, and service remained consistent. Once waiters stopped working at the restaurants where they were trained and became transient, styles of service began to blend together. Everyone took the best parts of a particular service and adapted it to his restaurant. Many ideas about service were passed down correctly, but others were passed down incorrectly. Service is now beginning to be as important as cooking.

Throughout the United States and Canada, there is no definitive type of service. Each restaurant has its own style of service. There are three basic kinds of service used in a la carte restaurants. These are American, French, and Russian. Most restaurants use a combination of all three to serve their guests. Many restaurant personnel have a basic understanding of the three types of service. However, they are not certain about the advantages and disadvantages of each particular service. Likewise, many people are confused concerning the difference between Russian banquet service and French service. Buffet service includes three other types of service, which adds to the confusion. Overall, there is a lot of misinformation about the origins and the exact definition of the different types of service.

In the years 1000-1500 A.D., travellers would stop for food and lodging at inns and taverns in France and England. Everyone had the same meal served to them. This one choice, a complete meal, was and is still called table d'hote. In 1533, La Tour d'Argent opened in Paris, France. This was the first restaurant open to the public in the Western world. Guests at La Tour could order their own individual meals from a menu for the first time. French Service

The first meals served in France were done so with considerable flourish and show. The meal was divided into three separate services. Hors d'oeuvres were served first. Then came the first service. Everything that the guests ate was placed in the dining room on tables and warmers (like today's buffet). Each guest was waited on by a server (called a valet) or two. The valet assisted the guests by obtaining the food for them. Guests, while seated, could serve themselves from the offered dish, but forks, spoons, or knives because the only utensils put on the table were spoons. There were no napkins to fold and put on the table, since each guest was required to bring his own cloth to wipe his hands. The servants' job was not without danger. In addition to obtaining food and drink for their masters and peeling their grapes, they tasted the food and drink to make certain that they were not poisoned. If the taster ate the food and lived, then the master ate it.

The Roman people were very superstitious. Guests were seated at a single couch with as few as three or as many as thirty people. The key was to have a multiple of three because that number held divine significance. All guests made certain to enter the banquet hall with their right foot first. This assured them that favourable things would happen to them. Emperor Augustus, the founder of the Roman Empire, gave women official status in Roman society around 27 B.C. He allowed women to accompany their husbands to banquets. Because there was a great amount of gossip at banquets, anything that was said at the table was not repeated if the host put a rose on the table. This led to the terms sub rosa, which means confidentiality.

Use of Knives

In the medieval times, knives were used for hunting and protection. Every man carried a knife with him. One of the uses for the knife, discovered by early man, was to spear his food with the pointed end. He could then transport the food to his mouth without using his hands. The inns and taverns in Europe that served food and drink did not provide their guests with any utensils, because they had their own. In addition, medieval times were dangerous; the patron of the inn was in a strange place, never knowing who might attack him. When the patron ate, if he had to lay his knife down on the table, he would put it on his right-hand side. Food and cooking became the rage in France. Any French person who wanted to be considered knowledgeable in the ways of the world learned about cooking.

The French palate was becoming sophisticated. Under the reigns of King Louis XIV and Louis XV, it became stylish to employ a famous chef. Families, like Bechamel, were proud to have a new sauce named after them. French people started to entertain more and service became an important element of the meal. Since so many people were becoming knowledgeable about food, service had to become creative to keep up with the new foods. Instead of food being prepared solely in the kitchen, it was prepared in front of the guests with a flourish. As the guests were now civilised, they had utensils to eat their food with besides their fingers.

Place Setting

In homes and restaurants, the standard placement of flatware (spoons, forks, knives) generally follows the same pattern. It has not changed substantially from the original place setting begun in the homes and restaurants of France. To the left side of the guest is placed the bread and butter dish, and forks. The knives, spoons, glasses, and cups are to the right. A napkin is placed in the center of the place setting.

Set the Table

Then the manager must be a stickler for detail by inspecting all tables and correcting mistakes before the banquet begins or the dining room opens. A manager will be able to walk into any room and know immediately what is correct and incorrect about the place settings. In time, setting the table properly will become second nature to the service staff. Generally, the utensil that will be used to eat the first course is placed the farthest from the guest. If soup were served first, the soup spoon would be the farthest spoon away from the guest's right hand. Next to the spoons are the knives.

All blades are pointed toward the forks or center of the place setting. Europeans cut their food with their knife held in their right hand. They eat their food holding the fork in their left hand. Americans have the habit of cutting the food the same way and then transferring the fork to their right hand before eating the food. Because of this European tradition, place settings continue to follow this general pattern. Above the tip of the dinner knife is the water glass. Next to the water glass is the wine glass. Because wine is considered a food in Europe and because it complements the meal, and in some countries water was not fit for human consumption, it is an important part of the meal. Because guests drank more wine than water (if it was served), the placement of the wine glass made it easy for the service person to pour the wine. On the left side of the place setting are the dinner and salad forks. Immediately above or to the left of the forks is the bread and butter plate. The distance between the forks and knives should be 12 inches at a banquet, 18 inches at an a la carte establishment.

Most service staff, after setting a table for a few days, are able to place the utensils perfectly on the table. There is an easy way for a service person to determine this distance at banquets. The service person should stand facing the table, with a knife in the right hand and a fork in the left hand. These utensils should be placed on the table in direct line with the shoulders. Most adults have shoulders approximately 12 inches wide. The utensils should be placed one inch from the edge of the table. Each restaurant can adapt its place settings to its menu, adding or subtracting utensils.

For instance, if all guests are served soup with their meal, then a soup spoon is added to the place setting. Notice that there is no coffee cup or saucer at the place setting. These are brought with the dessert course or when the guest orders coffee and placed to the right of the spoons. The handle on the coffee cup should be located in a position that would be the same as the hour hand on a clock pointing to the number five. This position is called "cup at five o'clock." This is strictly for guest comfort. When the guest reaches for the coffee cup, the handle of the cup will not have to be moved. The guest's fingers will fit perfectly into the handle. This is just another detail that will make a restaurant stand out from its competitors. Everything in the restaurant should be for the benefit and comfort of the guest.

During the period when kings were in power and the wealthy aristocrats were influential in France, all the skilled cooks, chefs, and valets were employed by these individuals. In 1789, a revolution took place; the royalty was overthrown and removed. As Napoleon gained power, it appeared that France's great culinary development would stop. This was a blessing in disguise for service. Because there was no more royalty, there was very little employment for the great cooks in the homes of wealthy people. The cooks had to find a new place to earn a living. Restaurants gave these cooks an opportunity for employment. Either the cooks worked for someone or opened up their own establishments. From 1765 until 1800, the number of restaurants increased from one to five hundred in Paris. The cooks introduced a new type of service to the French people, using their culinary skills to prepare meals in front of the guest.

French service as we know it today was born. Today's French service is characterised by a service person's finishing off (cooking, carving, flaming, and so on) the food in front of the guest the food is partially prepared in the kitchen and brought to the table on a cart, called a gueridon. On the gueridon is a small heating utensil, called a rechaud. The food will be prepared on this gueridon, using the rechaud for last-minute cooking in full view of the guests. Because the people doing the cooking at the table (after the French Revolution) were chefs, the job title of this service person is chef de rang. This person might be highly skilled in order to prepare utensils is a direct result of a right-handed society and European etiquette. When a service person notices (being ubiquitous) that the guest has moved the beverage glass to the left side, the coffee cup should be placed to the guest's left, with the handle at seven o'clock. French service has some excellent advantages:

1. The main advantage is for the guest, who gets a high degree of personal attention.
2. The service is showy and elegant.
3. Food is prepared with showmanship.
4. It may be possible to decrease the labour cost, because the chef and commis de rang are partially compensated with gratuities. Therefore, fully staffed, highly paid kitchen crew may not be needed.

However, there are more disadvantages than advantages for a restaurant in using French service:

1. The restaurant must employ highly skilled service staff, knowledgeable in cooking as well as service. They must know how to bone fish and poultry, carve meats, dress salads, and prepare flambe items. The chef de rang must be knowledgeable about ingredients and must have the personality to perform constantly. These individuals might be impossible to find in some areas of the country. Therefore, a well-planned training programme must be instituted and maintained.
2. If a restaurant does not have a good training programme, and even if it does, there could be a problem with consistent quality of food pre-pared by all the chef de rangs at all the tables. It becomes difficult to enforce standardised recipes and to correct

mistakes. Thus, the guests may get different quality food at different visits.

3. Because cooking is done in the dining room, the air may become stale with the odor of cooking unless the dining room has a good ventilation system.
4. Because gueridons must be used, a restaurant using French service will have less space for tables. French service requires 18 square feet per guest, while other services only require 15.
5. It costs more to buy and maintain the gueridons and rechauds. Other equipment must also be purchased which may not have to be purchased using American or Russian service.
6. It takes longer to serve guests using French service. A restaurant cannot serve as many guests in an evening. Generally, restaurants with this type of service have only one sitting a night. Or they have an early and late sitting, if the demand is great.
7. The cost of the meal must be high enough to cover all the above costs. Therefore, restaurants that use French service have to charge considerably more for a meal than those that use any other type of service.

The cuisine of Russia was greatly influenced by the French. Catherine the Great (1'762-1'796), one of the rulers of Russia, imported French chefs and corresponded regularly with Voltaire. She was a great Francophile. In turn, the service in French restaurants was influenced by the Russians. Because the Russians did not have many skilled chefs, the food served to wealthy aristocrats was prepared in the kitchen, rather than in front of the guests. To make the food look as appealing as possible, it was served on royalty's best serving pieces: silver trays. As the rulers of the two countries became allies, each country influenced the other. When the French returned home from Russia, they brought with them an idea for a new type of service to be used in restaurants. This new style of service in France was referred to as silver service.

When this new type of service was introduced to French restaurants, it revolutionised the industry. It became popular in the mid-1800s. No longer did restaurants have to find talented chefs to prepare food at the table-nor did they need gueridons. Now food could be served more quickly to more guests. Russian service is characterised by food being cooked and pre-portioned in the kitchen. All the food for a table is presented to the guests on silver trays. The service person then serves the food to the guests' plate from the tray.

In the United States and Germany this service is called Russian. A more casual example would be family style service. In France, because it originated in French restaurants, it is called French or silver service. Russian service has many advantages over French service for a restaurant owner or manager. It is best used for banquets rather than for a la carte service.

— Food portioned and arranged on a silver platter looks appealing, and impressive.

— Less space is required than for French service, because gueridons are not needed; therefore, more tables can be placed in the dining room, resulting in more meals served.

— Guests will be more comfortable at the table, because 30 inches of linear space are needed for Russian service, as opposed to 24 inches for other services.

— Guests can be served more quickly, which allows for more turnover than does French service.

— The service staff do not have to be skilled in food preparation.

— The quality control can be better maintained than with French service, because all food is cooked and put on platters in the kitchen.

Russian service does have some disadvantages:

- — A service person has to be skilful in manipulating a fork and spoon to transfer food from the platter to the guest's plate.
- — All tables must be located so that they can be easily served. If a table is located too close to a wall, it becomes impossible to serve a guest.
- — When guests order different entrees it requires bringing different platters to the table. This is time consuming. The first guest served will end up with cold food to eat if he or she waits for all the guests to be served.
- — There is a high initial cost for purchasing the silver platters. A larger problem is controlling the inventory of silver and preventing theft.
- — If all guests order the same entree, the last person served could find the look of the food picked over and unappealing.

Place Settings

Because the two types of service are so similar, the place settings are identical. The difference between this setting and the basic setting is that the dessert fork and spoon are already on the table. One other difference is that the knife is on the bread and butter plate. Notice the placement of the glasses. There should never be more than three glasses at a place setting.

Spoons: The spoon is the oldest of all eating utensils. It is also the simplest. The earliest ones were made out of wood. The Egyptian spoons were carved from ivory and wood or various metals. Elaborately shaped handles were designed and were often decorated with lotus blossoms. The spoon was a mark of class in medieval society. Each person brought his or her own set of utensils to dinner.

Children were given their own set when they were old enough to eat with company. The expression "to be born with a silver spoon in your mouth" came about because wealthy families started the practice of giving a set of spoons to their children at birth. This phrase meant that the children came from a well-to-do family. Russian and French place settings are identical. The setting is basically the same as American style, except for a dessert soon and dessert fork placed above the center of the place setting.

Cesar Ritz: Russian service, as well as French, was being experienced by more guests. More restaurants were finding that Russian service was more economical to use. Waiters did not get as much respect as the talented chef de rangs of French service. Cesar Ritz is credited with making serving guests a profession. Cesar lived from 1850 to 1918. His great learning took place when he worked as a commis de rang (assistant waiter) at the most famous restaurant in Paris, the Viosin. He took the job at Voisin so he could learn the best methods in serving techniques. He learned to deal well with people, and was so responsive to their wishes that before loner guests were insisting on being served by him. He was a master at details. Soon he was in demand to manage restaurants and hotels all over Europe. Ritz changed the setting of the party and the menu to give the guests the impression of warmth.

The forty-seat table was moved into a small room and covered with a red tablecloth. Four large copper bowls were filled with methylated spirits; when the guest arrived it was lit. For each guest a hot brick was wrapped in a flannel cloth and placed under his or her feet. The guests began the meal with a hot consomme and ended with crepes flambees. Because of this obsession with details, the guests had no complaints about the temperature and the luncheon was a success. Ritz's name and fame soon spread. His treatment or guests and his staff's service was legendary. He and Escoffier (the great French chef) began working together. Ritz would be in charge of the service, Escoffier of the kitchen. Escoffier created new dishes and named them for a favoured few of their customers. Ritz chose the customers. Peach Melba, Melba toast, and Sauce Melba were created and named for the great Australian opera singer Dame Nellie Melba. His waiters were taught to give dignified service. They served in silence but were always at hand when needed. The dining room was always planned to he elegant and attractive enough to attract the most elegant of ladies.

As Ritz made it a policy to have elegant surroundings for his restaurants, modern restaurant managers should also have standards for their establishment. Every restaurant and banquet house has a place setting on the table before the guests eat their meal. Our place settings are different from those of Ancient Rome and of medieval times. Some establishments have opulent linens, silver, and crystal, while others have only the bare essentials. The area or space for all utensils (including salt, pepper, and ashtrays) for each guest is called the cover. Many people refer to this as the place setting. However, note that the place setting includes only the utensils for the guest to eat the meal, while the cover includes all the space for each guest.

A restaurant manager should make sure that each cover is set consistently. This is another factor that distinguishes an award-winning restaurant from others. With any style of service, enough space must be allowed so that guests are not crowded and service staff can serve them safely. French and American services require 24 linear (straight line) inches of space for guest comfort; Russian service requires 30 inches. All should have an area 15 inches deep. Therefore, in American banquet service, a table that is 8 feet long by 3 feet wide can seat four guests on each side of the table, for a total of eight guests. Regardless of the size of the table, the manager must make sure that both the guests and service staff have enough room so the guest can be comfortable and the service staff can serve properly.

Some restaurants will use a placemat to cover the area for the place setting; others will use a tablecloth; still others use a table-cloth covered by a glass top. Originally, restaurants that used placemats were usually low-priced coffee shops. Today, more and more restaurants (regardless of the type or the price of the meal) are choosing placemats rather than cloth because they are less expensive. The placemats range in quality from paper to plastic or cloth. The placemat should be set about 2 inches from the edge of the table. The utensils go on the placemat. Tablecloths are used for most banquets and, generally, in restaurants that have a high check average.

Tablecloths should be placed on tables in banquet rooms by two people. The service persons stand on either side of the table while unfolding the tablecloth and laying it on the table. Tablecloths should be hung even with the seat of the chair. In an a la carte restaurant, one person can place the cloth on the table, because the tables are smaller. In an a la carte restaurant, it may become necessary to change the cloth without exposing the bare tabletop to the guests. Changing a cloth should be done discreetly, without a flourish that would distract the guests.

Glass tops: Some restaurants have discovered a new way to cut costs while still using tablecloths to make the restaurant look nice. The table is covered with a tablecloth, then a glass top (which has been specially made for each table) is placed over the cloth. The cover may be set directly on top of the glass. One disadvantage is that the glass has to be cleaned with a glass cleaner after every meal. The smell of the cleaner might be offensive to some guests. Another disadvantage is that the use of glass tops adds to the noise level in a restaurant. To complete the cover the table is finally set with a napkin, either cloth or paper. The napkin should be the last item placed on the table.

Dining in America was affected by the Puritan influence. There was only one purpose for eating: to refuel the body. To dine or enjoy the meal was thought to be bad. The restaurant business in America got its start in the 1800s at taverns and roadhouses. Service at the beginning of this century was be correct. The napkin can go in the center of the place setting, in a water glass, or in the center of the starter plate (for establishments that use a starter plate). The napkins should not go under the forks. Depending on the policies of the restaurant, management may have the napkins folded in an artistic manner.

American service was and is still characterised by "Food on the plate, no wait." This was the American custom. All food was put on one plate and served to the guest, as opposed to French service, where separate plates for vegetables were used. All guests sat in a common room and ordered from a very limited menu. Large quantities of food were served to the guest. The eating hours were set for the convenience of management. During the 1830s, a great influx of French immigrants entered America, bringing their way to serve food. At about the same time, many German and Italian waiters and cooks came to the United States, because they had heard that the streets were paved with gold. They also brought with them a better style of service than was available in America. As they found employment in America, they introduced their methods of service in the places where they worked. Eventually, service got better and a style of service began to develop.

Another reason that'service got better was that employers went to Europe and got entire kitchen and dining room staffs to come to America. The owners paid for the workers' trip over. This was a way to get to those gold-paved streets. The owners would offer to pay wages to the cooks, but told the service staff they could work only for tips. Restaurant owners did this to cut down on their labor costs. It worked; many people were looking to go to the new world, and they were pleased to have the opportunity. America had always been tipless.

When the owners returned from Europe with their new staffs, they introduced tipping into America-claiming it was an established European practice. At the same time that the great influx of immigrants were arriving in the United States, Delmonico's opened in New York City. This restaurant gets the credit for teaching the American public how to enjoy fine dining. It also set the standard for elegance that all other restaurants in the United States tried to match. Delmcnico's offered the first a la carte menu, courteous service, private dining rooms, flowers, music, and fine wines to its guests.

American service is characterised by portioning all the food on the dinner plate in the kitchen. It is also referred to as plate service or German service. It is the fastest of all types, and requires the least amount of skill to wait on guests. One service person generally works a station (a group of tables in an area of the room) containing between fourteen to eighteen seats. The main difference in serving food in American service, as opposed to French and Russian service, is that all food is served from the guest's left side with the service person's left hand, and all beverages are served from the guest's right side with the service person's right hand.

Raymond J. Goodman theorises in his book *The Management of Service* that the practice of serving food from the guest's left side occurred because Americans consume more beverages and more varieties of beverages than Europeans.' Because the glasses are positioned on the right of the place setting, it was easier to serve the food from the left side, so as not to disturb the guest when he was drinking or reaching for his glass. The advantages of American service far outweigh the disadvantage:

1. It is a simple service to teach and learn. The staff only has to put a plate in front of the guest. They do not have to know how to cook, carve, or flambe.
2. A skilled staff is not necessary. Almost anyone can be trained to serve American style.
3. The cost of equipment is small, as there are no gueridons or silver trays to purchase.
4. Service is extremely fast.
5. Less dining room space is required for each guest.
6. Because service is fast and less space is required per guest, more guests can be served during the meal period.
7. Menu prices can be lower for the same meals compared to other services.
8. Portion and quality control are excellent, as all foods are plated in the kitchen.

There is just one main disadvantage in using American service: the service is not as elaborate as the other two American service is widely used in restaurants around the world today because the advantages far outweigh the disadvantages. Most restaurant managers will borrow parts of French and Russian service and incorporate it into their particular service style. For example, many restaurants in the United States offer salads made tableside (French); or they may serve a dish like lobster Newburg, portioning it out in front of the guests (Russian). American service is the best type of service to use for most restaurants.

BANQUET SERVICES

A banquet is a meal where all the food has been preselected by the host before the guests enter the room. Banquets are served using American, Russian, or buffet style. All have advantages and disadvantages. The key factor in serving banquets is that the service person have as much needed equipment on the guests' table before they enter the room. The purpose of banquets is to serve guests faster than in a la carte dining. This is because most banquets are arranged for a special purpose-a dance, testimonial, or awards presentation-not just to eat. Like American service, this is an easy service to serve. One waiter can usually serve from sixteen to twenty-four guests. The service is the same as American, except for the place setting. The place setting for American banquet service is similar to American a la carte service. However, the place setting changes with every banquet. A separate utensil is needed for each course. Because the purpose of the banquet is to serve guests as quickly as possible, the utensils should be preset.

The first types of forks had two prongs. They were used to hold sacrificial meat, not for eating. People ate by picking the food up with their fingers or the pointed end of a knife. Two people are credited with introducing the fork to modern society. A Byzantine princess introduced the fork in the eleventh century to the people of Venice, Italy. Queen Catherine de Medici was the second person. She introduced it to the aristocrats of France after returning from Italy in the mid-1500s. At first, it was used more as an amusement than as a serious eating utensil.

By the 1600s, forks became fashionable and were more acceptable than eating with one's fingers. Like spoons, forks became very elaborate. These forks sometimes were as elaborate as a piece of jewellery. When people were invited to dinner, they carried their precious forks with them in special cases. Forks were introduced to England by Tomas Coryate, who brought back samples of them from Italy, where he first used them.

Russian banquet service is the most elegant of banquet services. Two service people are generally assigned to work in pairs, serving a total of twenty guests. Food is served from platter to plate. One server serves the main course, while the other follows with the potatoes and vegetables. A skilled staff is needed for this type of service. Like the American setting, all utensils are put on the table. However, each guest has his own set of salt and pepper shakers. The dessert fork and spoon are set above the place setting. As in American banquet service, the amount of silverware needed changes with each banquet, depending on the menu.

Buffet Service

Buffet service is characterised by the guests obtaining either their whole meal or parts of the meal from food that is displayed in the dining room. One service person can be assigned as many as thirty-five guests. The place settings for banquets have only enough utensils set to do the job. There are three types of buffets. The first is simply called buffet. In this service, guests obtain all their own food and drinks. The service person has only one job: to clean up dirty dishes. The second is called modified deluxe buffet. Tables are set with utensils and guests are served coffee, and perhaps dessert, by the service person. The third is the most elegant, called deluxe buffet. The guests are served the first and second course, as well as their beverages and dessert. They obtain their main course from an elegant buffet.

The service person must serve and clear many courses. They must have all the dirty plates cleared before the guest returns from the buffet table. One service person is needed for twenty guests in this style of buffet service. Because it is a banquet, the place setting of the buffet is determined by what food is offered on the buffet. Management should train their staff not to allow guests to bring back used plates and utensils to the buffet line. Instead, the guests should be given a new plate each time they come to the buffet line.

10

Waiter Service

As a waiter or waitress you serve food and drink to diners at their table. Your tasks would vary depending on the establishment you work in, but all include taking orders and serving food and drink. Making customers feel welcome and comfortable is an essential part of the job. To do this work you should have a welcoming, friendly attitude, a good memory, a high standard of personal hygiene and should be well turned out. You also need excellent communication skills and basic mathematical skills for calculating bills.

Working hours vary, but usually include evenings, weekends, public holidays and shift work. Overtime, part-time and seasonal work might be available. You will be on your feet all the time in warm, often hot conditions. Waiters and waitresses serve food in restaurants and other dining establishments. Depending on the size and type of restaurant, waiters and waitresses have a variety of job duties. Waiters and waitresses take orders for food and drinks. They describe daily specials and are sometimes asked to suggest an item on the menu or explain how an item is prepared. After writing down or memorising orders, waiters and waitresses relay orders to the kitchen staff or enter them into computers.

Waiters and waitresses serve beverages. If ordered, they serve appetizers, salads, or soups before the main course. Waiters and waitresses observe customers to make sure they have everything they need. They refill water glasses or other beverage items when needed. They also watch to determine when each course has been completed. Waiters and waitresses describe and take orders for dessert. They sometimes bring a tray containing a serving of each dessert special to customers' tables. When the meal is complete, waiters or waitresses remove the dishes and glasses from the table and take them to the kitchen. They compute the cost of the meal and prepare the check. They also accept payments or refer customers to the cashier. After customers have left, waiters or waitresses may replace the table linen and service. They refill salt, pepper, sugar, cream, and condiment containers. They also clean and arrange work stations, chairs, and table pieces.

In more expensive restaurants, headwaiters may greet and direct customers to tables. Headwaiters also take reservations over the phone and supervise other staff. To work as a waiter or waitress, you need:

a) on-the-job training;

b) excellent communication skills; and

c) work experience in a restaurant.

There are no formal education requirements beyond high school. However, some professional technical schools offer special training. Formal restaurants may require experience in food service. Informal restaurants are less likely to require experience. Most waiters and waitresses learn their skills on the job from an experienced worker. Some restaurants offer their own training program. Training includes: job duties; and restaurant policies. Training may last up to a month.

As the world moved into the Industrial Revolution in the 1800s, the world of food service moved quickly to fulfill the needs of workers. Factories drew large numbers of workers who had to be fed. The tight mealtime schedules caused a need for fast, efficient service. Counter service became popular, and the first Horn & Hardart Automat opened in Philadelphia in 1902. Fine dining wasn't dead, though. Delmonico's had a 100-page menu with 370 dishes and catered to New York's elite. In less than a century, fine food service went from being the province of the wealthy and powerful to being much more egalitarian and democratic.

As Americans continue to seek out sources of prepared food, food service will become increasingly part of their lives. This is a very popular style of service used not just in America but in many other countries. Its hallmark is efficiency, and thus it tends to be used in more casual and high-volume restaurants. Its efficiency has, though, attracted many purveyors of fine dining and led to its use in many formal restaurants. In American service, the food is cooked and plated in the kitchen. The waiter delivers the food, one plate at a time, to the guests at the table, ladies first. These days, most service professionals agree that the guest should be served from the right side, with the waiter's right hand.

Clearing of plates is also performed with the right hand from the right side. When the right hand is used for serving or clearing, the waiter should move around the table in a clockwise direction; it is more efficient (and safer) because the waiter is, by definition, walking forward rather than backing up. Conversely, any task performed with the left hand should lead the waiter around the table in a counterclockwise direction. In most American restaurants, the service brigade consists of waiters, runners, and bussers. The waiter interacts directly with the guests and manages his or her station.

Runners bring food from the kitchen into the dining room, and bussers clear and reset tables, pour water, refill bread, and assist the runner. Rather than threeperson teams, most restaurants have more waiters than runners, and more runners than bussers. This is because the runners' and bussers' jobs are more general and can cover more territory in the restaurant-their work isn't as guest-specific. Originally, French service was used with meals that consisted of three courses, one of which was already set on the table when guests entered the room. Subsequent courses were brought into the room on silver platters and served from gueridons. Between courses, the guests would get up from the table and it would be cleared-not exactly a turn-and-burn. While the current incarnation of French service is not quite as time-consuming as the original, this style has been relegated to the formal dining rooms of a few restaurants and hotels around the world.

Service Personnel

Not only does it require a large amount of expensive equipment, there is also the need for a highly trained service brigade to carry it out. This brigade is made up of the following personnel:

The Captain

The captain almost never leaves the dining room. He or she is always in sight of the guests and is their main contact. The captain takes most of the orders, prepares the tableside items, and runs the station with the assistance of the rest of the team. The captain must have a profound knowledge of food and wine and be able to translate that knowledge into language that is understandable to each and every guest. As a mixture of salesperson, confidant, and advocate, the captain is the most influential person with regard to the quality of the guest's dining experience.

The Front Waiter

The front waiter is the captain's lieutenant. His or her duties include regular table maintenance such as pouring water and clearing plates, as well as assisting the captain with tableside cooking and tending to the guests while the captain is occupied, either at the gueridon or at another table. Occasionally, the front waiter will take drink or dessert and coffee orders, but the dinner order (because of its importance and intricacy) is usually taken by the captain. The front waiter helps to coordinate the delivery of food to the table with the back waiter; the same team does most of the table clearing as well. The front waiter's position may not be as glamorous as that of the captain, but the captain relies heavily on the front waiter's efficacy.

The Black Waiter

The black waiter is also sometimes called a runner, but the terms aren't exactly equivalent. A runner is someone who brings food from the kitchen anywhere in the dining room. A back waiter, though, is part of a team that is responsible for a specific set of tables and brings food from the kitchen to those tables. In addition to running food, the back waiter will assist the front waiter as needed, perhaps pouring water, serving bread, clearing tables, and the like. So a true back waiter does more than just run food; he or she is responsible to the service team.

Busser or Guard

Busser or Guard is a position that some people, unfortunately, look down upon. Needless to say, the busser is an extremely valuable member of the service team and can be integral to that team's success. Primary responsibilities include basic table maintenance (bread and water), clearing, and the resetting of recently vacated tables. A great busser can lighten the burden on the rest of the service team, enabling them to concentrate more on serving the guests.

In French service the various staffers have to work as a team. Each member has both primary responsibilities and secondary responsibilities-for example, the captain will sometimes pour water when the front waiter is helping the back waiter deliver food to a table. The captain, though, should not be running food from the kitchen to the dining room unless the situation is dire. The hierarchy of the classic service team works very well, but there are limitations.

First of all, the restaurant has to be big enough that four-person teams can fit in the dining room. Second, the prices have to be high enough that all the members of a four-person team can make enough money to live on. Definitions of Russian service vary, but the most common involves platters of food being prepared in the kitchen and brought to the table, with the server placing the food on the guest's plate from the left side with the right hand. Sauce and garnish are served either by that waiter or by another one following right behind.

Advantages of this model include the relatively quick and personal service of hot food to a large number of guests. It also shows off the abilities of the service staff with relatively simple training. One disadvantage is that servers have to learn how to use the service spoon and fork in combination as a sort of tongs. Also, by the time the waiter gets to the last guest at the table, the platter can start looking a bit ragged. Portion control can be a bit tricky, especially if a guest asks for additional food, leaving the waiter without enough food for everyone at the table.

This rarely happens, though, so the other two potential problems loom a bit larger. These days, it is rather common for waiters in many types of dining rooms to use Russian service to place bread on guests' plates. Additionally, being handy with serviceware can be helpful when splitting menu items onto two plates for guests, either on the gueridon, on the side stand, or at the table.

Butler service: Take Russian service and let the guests serve themselves from the platter. That's butler service. The service utensils are on the platter for the guest to use, and the waiter still walks around the table counterclockwise, serving to the guests' left side.

English service: Essentially, it is Thanksgiving dinner in a restaurant. The food is fully cooked in the kitchen and sent out on platters to the dining room. The host carves the meat or plates the main course and hands the plates to the guests, who pass the plates around the table. Side dishes are sent out for the guests to help themselves, but the wait staff performs the other aspects of table maintenance. It would be used in a country club or some other venue where the guest wanted to mimic a home-style setting while still being waited on.

Family service: Family-style service is quite popular in some value-oriented restaurants, and also in places where the style fits with the theme. For instance, some Italian restaurants feature large platters of food that are brought to the table, where the guests serve themselves onto empty extra plates. It is a remarkably efficient style of service that can make a lot of sense (and money) for you in the right situation. The waiter's job is made easier in a number of ways: the order is easier to take, the food is easier to deliver, and individuals largely take care of themselves.

The kitchen is also helped by the fact that a table of four can be served with three large platters of food instead of four appetizers and four main courses-three large plates of food take much less time to prepare than eight single servings. Family-style service can be used in other types of casual restaurants. Customers enjoy the chance to serve themselves, it can lighten the burden in both the dining room and kitchen, and it can lower labor costs. As you can see, house style can function in two ways-both as a marketing tool, to attract a certain type of clientele (for example, businesspeople, or teens out with their friends), and as a way of creating regular business, by enticing back people who feel comfortable there. To be successful, any business must establish and maintain a consistent level of quality. On any given night, customers should be able to walk into a restaurant and experience the type of hospitality the restaurant has established a reputation for.

In the restaurant business, as in any field from sports to media to manufacturing, reliability and consistency are achieved through training and practice.To take a very different example, in basketball a winning team will always have more than one player who can be counted on to score free throws consistently, especially when the game is on the line, and that sort of consistency is due almost exclusively to hard work and practice between games.

In the restaurant business, a successful restaurant has a trained staff who not only can manage an average night in a way that keeps customers satisfied but also can handle just about anything that's thrown their way, such as a large last-minute party with many special requests on a busy night, an equipment malfunction in the kitchen, even a waiter suddenly becoming ill and other staff having to pitch in to cover his or her tables. Occasional flashes of brilliance are all well and good, perhaps drawing a lot of attention from food critics, but making quality a habit-establishing a routine so that every guest is greeted warmly within thirty seconds of entering the restaurant, giving waiters the information they need about the food so that guests'questions about the menu can be answered on the spot, making sure the dining room illumination and temperature are always at specified levels-is what brings customers back. While, hospitality is a concept that depends on feelings and impressions, the essence of service resides in action.

Service is being able to carry four dinner plates without spilling the sauce, or open-ing a bottle of Champagne without spewing foam onto the floor. Restaurateurs do these things to make people feel comfortable and attended to. While the tasks themselves do not involve emotion, they enable it, in the sense that carrying them out in a professional manner evokes positive feelings in guests. Satisfying the instinctual need to take nourishment is the reason people eat. There are many factors that contribute to the rise in dining out, such as increasingly busy schedules, greater mobility, and larger amounts of disposable income, but a primary answer is that dining out feels good: nice people bring you delicious things to eat and drink, and then wash the dishes after you leave.

Towards Effective Service

The first step is to identify what feelings and experiences you want a guest in your establishment to have, and then determine what specific actions on the part of the staff will help to bring them about. A friend had invited a number of interesting people to dinner and spared no expense with regard to food and drink. Yet somehow the evening just didn't come together. None of the guests had ever met before that night, and the awkward silences were amplified by the absence of background music. While the food was of very high quality, the various menu items were all very complicated and difficult to eat, and they did not complement each other well.

The guests were left on their own to rummage through the fridge for any beverage other than water. Every minute felt like an hour, and many guests seemed vaguely ill at ease. Some quiet jazz on the stereo, a simple bar with some wine and mineral water, and a few changes to the menu would have enhanced the experience, making for a more relaxed, convivial atmosphere that would have encouraged us all to get to know each other. This, of course, was a home dinner party, but the lessons apply to the restaurant business as well. Specific actions can lead to desired feelings and emotions on the guest's part, and these actions can be singled out, defined, described, and put into simple, trainable terms-for example, anticipating the pace of a meal and bringing successive courses at just the right time, making suggestions of menu items that will complement dishes already ordered, and presenting the check at just the right time after the meal is done. Many of the actions that can result in a guest's satisfaction are simple enough that almost any employee could be trained to perform them.

11

MEAL SERVICES

Chefs, cooks, and food preparation workers may work to prepare, flavor, and cook many different kinds of foods ranging from soups, snacks, and salads to main dishes, sides, and desserts in food establishments such as restaurants. The primary responsibility of chefs and cooks is to create recipes and prepare meals. On the other hand, food preparation workers' tasks include: peeling and cutting vegetables, trimming meat, preparing poultry, maintaining cleanliness, and checking oven and stovetop temperatures.

Generally, chefs and cooks follow a recipe to prepare food by measuring, mixing, and cooking. They use an assortment of equipment including pots, pans, cutlery, ovens, broilers, grills, slicers, grinders, and blenders. Additionally, chefs and head cooks are in charge of directing other workers in the kitchen, estimating food necessities, and ordering materials.

Restaurants and food service establishments that are bigger usually obtain diverse menus and expanded kitchen staffs. They frequently have numerous chefs and cooks who are often called assistant or line cooks and less advanced kitchen workers which include food preparers. Each of the chefs and cooks work in a designated area, furnished with the types of equipment and ingredients for specific foods prepared in that area. Job titles are often associated with the main ingredient used or type of cooking, for example, vegetable cook, fry cook, or grill cook.

Executive chefs and head cooks organize and direct the kitchen which includes the staff and meals. Their responsibilities include: determining serving sizes, planning menus, ordering supplies for food, and supervising kitchen operations to make sure that the food quality and presentation is consistent. The terms chef and cook are often thought of as the same; however, they normally mirror the varying types of chefs and the arranged structure.

For example, executive chefs are responsible for merely everything regarding the food operations as well as sometimes supervising several kitchens of a hotel, restaurant group, or corporate dining operation. A chef de cuisine is over all operations of a single kitchen and reports to an executive chef. A sous chef, also called a sub chef, is just under the chef in ranking and will run the kitchen when he/she is gone. Usually, chefs have further training and higher skills than cooks. Several chefs achieve a well-known name for themselves and their kitchens through the good quality and unique nature of the food.

Most cooks' exact responsibilities are determined by several different aspects, such as the kind of restaurant they are employed by. For example, institution and cafeteria cooks generally work in the kitchens institutions, such as schools, cafeterias, businesses, and hospitals. They cook and offer a limited number of choices for entrees, vegetables, and desserts for meals. Conversely, restaurant cooks typically several types of dishes as they cook for individual orders. Short-order cooks work in restaurants and coffee shops where quick preparation time and fast service are the primary goal. They work on several orders simultaneously preparing foods like hamburgers, sandwiches, eggs, and French fries.

Fast-food cooks work in fast-food restaurants where a limited menu is used. They prepare and wrap up batches of foods like hamburgers and fried chicken, so that they may stay warm until being served. Private household cooks work in a home to prepare and cook food that is desirable and fitting to the client. They may maintain needed groceries and supplies, clean and wash the kitchen and supplies, and serve meals. Food preparation workers work under the supervision of chef and cooks to perform regular and repetitive tasks like preparing ingredients, peeling and slicing vegetables, putting together salads and other cold items, and preparing meat and poultry for cooking.

Further responsibilities include: figuring out size and quantity of ingredients, searching for pots and pans, and stirring and straining soups and sauces. They also clean work areas, equipment, utensils, dishes, and silverware. The type of food service establishment determines the type and quantity of food workers. Fast-food establishments where limited items are offered only need fast-food cooks. Little, full-service restaurants that provide casual dining usually offer a limited number items that are easy to prepare and complement then these items with short-order specialties and previously prepared desserts. Normally, a short-order cook and one or two other kitchen workers help a main cook in preparing all the food.

Grocery and specialty food stores hire chefs, cooks, and food preparation workers to create recipes and prepare to-go orders. Usually, main entrees, side dishes, salads, and further items are cooked and packaged in bulk and stored at the right temperature. Servers divide and wrap up items to meet a costumer's order.

Cooking Training

For the majority of fast-food or short-order cooks and workers who prepare food, modest culinary arts education or training is required, leaving most skills to be acquired on the job. Training normally begins with basic safety and sanitation guidelines and continues with training on food handling, preparation, and cooking procedures. A high school diploma is required for individuals aspiring to become professional chefs; however, it is not required for beginning-level jobs. Programs offer through high school or vocational schools may provide education in essential food safety and handling procedures as well as general business and computer classes for students want to manage or own a food establishment.

Several school districts, in compliance with State departments of education, give training through experience and summer camps for cafeteria workers who want to advance to cooks. Paid internships and summer employment are offered to beginners in this field through big corporations in the food services and hospitality industries. Internships can be beneficial, providing important experience and leading to placement in advanced chef training programs. It is mandatory for executive chefs and head cooks working in prestigious restaurants to have several years of experience and training as well as interest in cooking.

A few chefs and cooks may begin their preparation in programs at high schools or post-high school vocational schools. On the other hand, others receive the necessary training by attending independent cooking schools, professional culinary institutes, or colleges with 2 and 4-year to obtain a hospitality or culinary arts degree. Further, selective established hotels and restaurants train their own chefs and cooks through private programs. The majority of formal training programs mandate students participate in some kind of apprenticeship, internship, or out-placement program that are mutually offered by the school and associated restaurants. Formal apprenticeship programs are sponsored by professional culinary institutes, industry associations, and trade unions in accordance with the U.S. Department of Labor. Several receive valuable work experience and instruction as they are trained on-the-job from chef tutors in the restaurants.

TRAINING FOR SUPPLIERS

The waitress moved the menus and place settings to the new table. She then asked for their orders. They ordered salad and asked her what the salad dressing choices were. She said she didn't know because that was her first night on the job, though she had worked at the restaurant during the summer, before she went away to college. She asked the waitress next to her for the choice of salad dressings and then repeated them back to the guests. One of the guests was reading her menu and did not hear the choices. When she ordered her salad, the whole process had to be repeated, with their waitress again asking the other waitress the choice' of salad dressings. Five of the six meals were delivered to the table. The order for the first guest (the hamburger) was served on a bun.

There were three other meals, besides the hamburger, which were to receive French fries as an accompaniment. Each meal had on the plate, the sandwich, an orange garnish and a sprig of parsley, plus a large area of white space left on the plate. Five minutes later, the waitress brought a community basket of French fries to the table, explaining that they had not been ready when she had brought out the other food. The sixth meal was finally brought to the table along with the French fries. Coffee was asked for and brought. The coffee was served with a napkin between the cup and saucer. The coffee spilled all over the napkin. The waitress asked the customer if she wanted a new napkin. The customer felt like saying "No, I'd rather slop it over my dress."

Before a manager allows employees to wait on guests, there are many facts they should know. The first group of facts deals with specific policies about the restaurant. Acceptable standards of appearance, dress, and attendance should be explained before the service person has been hired. Additional items, such as what time to report to work, food and drink policies concerning consumption both on and off the job, and serving hours, should also be explained to the employees. These facts must be reinforced in a training booklet. The next set of facts should deal with the establishment.

The purpose of having these facts known is so the service people can answer any and all questions that guests ask. The guest will feel good about the service person if he or she is able to answer questions intelligently and confidently. A third group of facts should be concerned with the physical layout of the restaurant. It should also explain how to order and pick up food and beverages. There should be an area that explains how to write and read guest dinner checks. The list is long but important for a successfully run restaurant. Guests perceive service persons in two ways: Are they nice, and can they answer questions?

Guests will ask many questions. Most of them are legitimate, but others may seem silly. However, they are not silly to the guest. All of the employees must know the history of the business. For example, questions will be asked concerning the ownership of the restaurant; how long has it existed; and what are the names and locations of other restaurants in the chain. Other facts employees should know are the days and hours of operation of their restaurant. If there are any other restaurants on the premises or in the hotel, the employees should know their hours of operation, type of foods served, the general price range, and the dress code. There should be a daily listing stating what events are occurring in the restaurant, hotel, and community.

The manager should stress to the employees the correct way to write and read a guest check. The manager must translate all the menu items into standard abbreviations. Each item must have its own abbreviation. All employees (including kitchen staff) are required to know and use the abbreviations when ordering food from the kitchen or serving food. This is to prevent any confusion in the restaurant. For example, what does SS on the check mean? Would the guest receive shrimp scampi, sirloin steak, or swiss steak? Abbreviations are used for all menu items, including accompaniments. Many times restaurants offer a children's menu. With the advent of computerized systems, which transmit orders directly to the kitchen, does a service person still need to know the importance of using abbreviations?

Training for Menu Planning

Many times guests are not familiar with your menu, so they ask the service person about the entrees. For example, a guest will ask "What is the shrimp scampi?" The service person should know the names of all items, how to pronounce them, and how to describe them. The training manual should have a description of all menu items. Guests often inquire about terms on the menu that are unfamiliar to them. For instance, a guest may ask the meaning of saute. Each employee should know the more common preparation methods of cooking foods. There are at least twelve methods. This information is also needed in the manual.

An example of two cooking methods: Baked-cooked by dry, continuous heat in an oven; sauteed-browned or cooked in a small amount of hot fat. A chart of the cooking times of all menu items should be listed. The chart should range from Pittsburgh to well done, with the normal cooking time for each item.

As with the food, there should be a description of every beverage the restaurant has available. In addition, there should be a description of how the drinks are made, the glass the drink is served in, and the proper garnish. The brand names of all wines and beverages must also be included in the section on alcoholic beverages.

Because menus are constantly being changed, a separate price sheet should be distributed with the current prices. Owing to the fluctuation of prices, putting prices into the manual would be a waste of time and money. The prices will most likely change more often than any other information in the manual. When done on a separate sheet, the manager only has to print the new prices instead of the entire manual.

This is another part of the training for the service staff that must be continuous. However, many restaurant managers refuse to let their staff taste the food. Instead, they serve them an employee meal each evening. The feeling is that it is too expensive to serve to the staff. In reality, it is too expensive not to serve it to the staff. The guests are going to ask the service person how the food tastes. If they have never been allowed to sample the food, how will your service staff know what to tell the guests? The service staff should taste all food and beverage items as soon as it is practical.

This does not mean that each night, the service staff should have a gourmet meal; but they must taste the food that they will be recommending and serving to their guests. One way of accomplishing this is by having meetings where the service staff sample the menu items. Or management could encourage the service staff to entertain their families at the restaurant and purchase their meals at a discount. Once the service staff has mastered the knowledge concerning the restaurant and menu by the testing criteria set up, it is time for them to move on to the second part: serving the meal.

Food and Beverage Merchandising

Merchandising food and beverage is simply another term for selling. Selling occurs because the guest likes and is confident in the service person's ability. This part of the training programme should concentrate on getting the guests to like your staff. This should be done by placing the service staff in common situations that occur daily in the restaurant. This is called role playing. For instance, have the service staff ask the "guests" what type of salad dressing they want, using the example of the problem stated on the preceding page. The service person should assess the mood of the guests as they approach the table. Are they celebrating and in a festive mood or do they appear somber, as if they have just returned from a funeral? Once the service person has assessed the situation, the behaviour should be appropriate for the situation. Each guest deserves and expects a warm, sincere greeting. If the staff person knows the guest, the guest should be addressed by name.

Furthermore, the staff should acknowledge the presence of the guest immediately and take care of any requests as soon as possible. This will make the guest feel as if the restaurant appreciates his or her patronage and will help make the dining experience a positive one. Many times guests will know exactly what food they wish to order; other times they cannot make up their minds. There is a trick that experienced service persons use to sell items and help guests make up their minds.

If guests are asked for their order and they hesitate, count backwards from seven. If the guests have not made up their minds by the time the server reaches zero, then they need help. And that opens it up for the service staff to sell suggestively. The first step in suggestive selling is having the guests like the service person. Once this happens, the guests will respond to the service person's suggestions. The guests now trust the service person's knowledge and judgement. He or she has answered all the guests' questions about the restaurant, told them what is happening in the area, and is perceived as knowledgeable.

The service person may then describe a meal that tastes and looks great based upon their preference. This is the main reason why employees should be required to taste all items on the menu. They are then able to describe how the food tastes and can base their recommendations on what the guest desires. The key to suggestive selling is for the service person to keep a positive attitude. The staff must put themselves in their guests' place, then use mouth-watering descriptions of the menu item for the purpose of selling the item. If a service person does not suggest desserts, or merely asks the' guests if they care to see a dessert menu, too often the answer is "No." By suggesting a specific dessert and using mouth-watering descriptions, the rate of success of selling desserts will be greatly enhanced.

Another technique used by experienced salespeople is to suggest last the item they wish to sell. This is because people usually remember the last thing said to them. Suggestive selling can build the profits for the restaurant by encouraging guests to order extra items that they normally would not have ordered. It also builds up the check total; and as most guests tip on the total bill, the amount of tip for the service person increases.

Special Service

Contrary to that, it usually means a special item prepared by the chef. The price is special. In some areas it is lower priced, or "best buy," and in other areas it is higher than a normal menu item. A manager might do well to change the name of the special of the day to the chef's creation. Then the service staff can approach the table and explain the chef's creation to the guests. Should the service staff be instructed to inform the guests of the price of the chef's creation? No one has ever satisfactorily explained the reason why prices are not given when a special item is offered. This is another positive factor that builds up the trust of the guest. Another annoying custom is for restaurants to instruct their service staff to offer an item (such as blue cheese dressing), and state it is "a la carte." Most guests have no idea what a la carte means.

The service staff should inform the guests the price of all items. Other techniques may assist the service staff in selling additional items in a restaurant. These are usually associated with wine and dessert sales. More and more restaurants include wine glasses at the place setting. Others sell a sample two-ounce portion of wine to the guests. Still others put a bottle of unopened wine on each table to encourage guests to order wine with their meal. Desserts provide the opportunity to increase sales enormously. Even though the American public is becoming more nutrition conscious and eating lighter meals, survey after survey has found that guests will order desserts.

Many restaurants display their desserts so the guests can view them before they begin their meal. This technique has been used successfully by many restaurants for merchandising desserts. If the desserts are kept attractive and eye-appealing, the guest will usually order dessert. However, if the cart or table becomes messy and unappetizing, it does the restaurant more harm than good.

Another excellent way to merchandise desserts is to bring out a sample tray of all desserts. The service person brings the trays to the guests' table and describes the desserts to them. This method eliminates the problem of the desserts looking unattractive, because the desserts on the tray are not served to the guests.

Instead, the service person obtains the desserts from the kitchen. As soon as a dessert on the tray looks unappealing, it is replaced. One of the best selling gimmicks that has been used for ages is initiated by the manager. If done properly, it can increase sales and repeat business dramatically. It involves the manager giving away an item that will call attention to that item. For example, a restaurant sells flaming coffee. The manager should approach a table in the center of the dining room, where other guests can see the coffee being prepared. The manager should introduce himself or herself to the guests, inquire about their meal, thank them for their business, and offer to buy them an after dinner coffee.

Once the coffee is being prepared, all, the eyes in the dining room are attracted to the coffee presentation. This display will encourage other guests to order the coffee after their meals. This can be done with a fancy dessert, large glass of beer, or any type of fancy entree. The cost of this to the restaurant is the cost of the item. In addition, the guest will feel special, because the manager gave away an item. The manager must encourage the service staff to sell extra items. The guests have already made the decision to patronize the restaurant. With suggestive selling, the service staff can increase profits for the restaurant. However, one word of caution: the manager must make certain that the service staff do no push so hard that the guests become upset with their selling aggressiveness and have a bad dining experience.

Training for Order Taking

Training your staff to take a guest's food and beverage order correctly is critical. There are many correct methods to take the order. All of them should have one goal: to serve the meal to the guest without having to ask who gets what. The manager should teach the service staff how to talk to the guests and how to take meal orders. The manager must impress upon the service staff that they should treat the guests as if they had never dined at the restaurant before. They do not know how the specials are made or what the salad dressing is that evening. It must be impressed upon the service staff that this will be the first time the guest hears the specials. Even though the service staff may have repeated them one hundred times that evening, employees should be taught to explain every item to each guest. The manager must train staff to explain in detail the chef's creation of the evening.

When it is time to offer the guest the choice of salad dressings or vegetables, explain what they are. Rather than let the staff say, "And what would you like on your salad?" encourage them to say something like: "A salad is included in the meal. Our choice of dressings are: blue cheese; Russian; Italian; and our house dressing, which is a sweet and sour dressing made with mustard and honey." The same should be true for vegetables, potatoes, and chef creations, especially if the item is new or one that is not normally served in the area where your restaurant is located. Included in the explanation can be the ingredients, how it is prepared, and the price. Finally, the order should be repeated back to the guest. By doing this, your service staff will avoid any misunderstandings of guest orders.

However, the method used should not be annoying to the guests. For instance, a service person who echoes every single item that the guest orders will be annoying. It is much better to wait until the complete order is taken and then repeat the main course back to the guest. The job of the service staff should not just be to serve the food, but to be the human link between the kitchen and the guest. This is why the importance of verbal communication between the service staff and the guest must be stressed. It gives the restaurant a personality.

There are two opinions on where the service persons should be standing when they take the guests' order. Both agree that order taking should follow the proper guidelines of service: children first, then women, then men. There is an exception, when one person is the host of the party and he or she is ordering for the entire table. The first method states that the service person should stand to the left of the guest and take the order, then move to the next person, following the proper guidelines of service, and take the order. The problem with this method is that if the service person takes the order by following proper guidelines, it may be necessary to skip over one male guest to take the next female's order.

The service person will then have to return to the man, and move back and forth, creating much unnecessary confusion. The second method is to have the service person stand in one spot and take all the guests' orders from that spot, following the proper guidelines of service. This works well at a table with two to four guests. However, for more than four guests, especially with rectangular-shaped tables, the service person may have to move to different spots in order to hear the order. Whichever method is used, the management should set guidelines for their own restaurant, keeping in mind that guests should be served smoothly and efficiently.

Training for Writing Orders

Once the staff know where the home base is, the next thing the manager must teach them is how to write the guest orders. The system must be explained simply enough so that any employee who picks up the food order can deliver it to the guests without having to ask who gets what. Each person should be provided with some sort of form with which to take orders. The service person must be organized; but it is up to the manager to devise this policy in such a way that all employees will know who gets what item. Some restaurants use a system that has the guest check remain at the table, in a slot provided in each table. The duplicate check (dupe) is brought into the kitchen to order the food. The guest check can have the system of "who gets what" directly written on the check.

The service staff will write the check in the following manner: The seat immediately to the left of the slot is the number 1 seat. Going in a clockwise direction, the seats are numbered consecutively, 2, 3, 4. The management arranges the tables so that the slots are always in the same position relative to the home base. These are two methods for writing guest orders and determining who gets what order. There are other methods, but they all have one thing in common: They are set up in an organized manner than can be easily learned. The key is to have the manager decide on one system and have all of the staff use the same system.

Code order system: Another system for determining who gets what is the code order. This system is not recommended, because too much confusion and embarrassment can result. The code order system was used in the past when a single service person was responsible for the station. The service person would write next to the order a code to identify the guest. The code would represent some distinguishing feature that made one guest stand out from the other, such as blue tie or red hair. This system can create problems because not all the service staff would understand the system. It also could be embarrassing if the service person uses a code order that was derogatory toward the guestsuch as fat person, bald, or grey hair.

Correct ordering in the kitchen is a must for guests to receive their dinner cooked and served properly. As the service staff know the time it takes to cook every item, they should submit their orders based on the mood of the guests and how long it will take to cook the meal. In most restaurants, the time to submit the order is when the service person picks up the guests' salad from the kitchen. In restaurants with a salad bar, the service person is instructed to turn the order into the kitchen when the guests go to obtain their salads from the salad bar. However, each manager can determine what is best for his or her individual unit. Depending on the type of system, the service persons may be required to order all the entrees at the top of their check. They may put all the cold items at the bottom. Others may have a computerized system that prints all the orders in a priority based on cooking times.

Training for Serving the Meal

If the meal is served incorrectly, the evening can be ruined. The service staff has ordered the meal correctly. It has been cooked properly, and the kitchen is waiting for the service person to serve it to the guest in the dining room. But instead of being picked up and delivered to the guest, it sits in the kitchen, becoming colder and less appetizing. Timing is of the essence. The staff must get the meal to the table as soon as it is ready. If the dinners sit too long, the quality suffers, and the guests become impatient. More and more restaurants are using electronic means to notify the service person that the meal is ready. These electronic devices may include a light system, a vibrating beeper, or other methods to let the service person know that the order is ready to be picked up.

As soon as the food is ready, the service person should pick it up and bring it to the table. But before doing so, the service person should take a few seconds to check that all the food items on the dupe match those that have been prepared by the kitchen. He or she must also check to see that all special instructions on the dupe have been followed. The tray will be loaded by placing the cold items first, then the hot items. The food on the tray should be arranged to serve the guests in the most efficient manner. Any condiments and garnishes should be brought to the guests' table along with the entrees.

12

Food Service Management

Restaurants, hotels and other food service industries often employ three distinct types of employees—chefs, cooks, and food preparation workers.

— Chefs are responsible for directing the activities of other kitchen workers, menu planning, recipe creation, food and supply ordering, and some specific cooking duties. They are typically the most senior members of the staff.

— Cooks are responsible for the day to day food preparation at the restaurant or facility. Depending on the size of the facility, there may be several cooks, each responsible for a different part of the menu, or a different type of food. For example, there are fry cooks, vegetable cooks, pastry cooks, and other specialities.

— Food preparation workers work under the supervision of chefs and cooks, and typically perform less skilled duties. For example, they may chop vegetables, prepare salads, and prepare materials used by the restaurant's chefs and cooks.

Chefs, Cooks, and Food Preparation Workers

Chefs, cooks, and food preparation workers prepare,

season, and cook a wide range of foods-from soups, snacks, and salads to entrees, side dishes, and desserts-in a variety of restaurants and other food services establishments. Chefs and cooks create recipes and prepare meals, while food preparation workers peel and cut vegetables, trim meat, prepare poultry, and perform other duties such as keeping work areas clean and monitoring temperatures of ovens and stovetops. In general, chefs and cooks measure, mix, and cook ingredients according to recipes, using a variety of pots, pans, cutlery, and other equipment, including ovens, broilers, grills, slicers, grinders, and blenders.

Chefs and head cooks also are responsible for directing the work of other kitchen workers, estimating food requirements, and ordering food supplies. Larger restaurants and food services establishments tend to have varied menus and larger kitchen staffs. They often include several chefs and cooks, sometimes called assistant or line cooks, along with other lesser skilled kitchen workers, such as food preparation workers. Each chef or cook works an assigned station that is equipped with the types of stoves, grills, pans, and ingredients needed for the foods prepared at each station.

Job titles often reflect the principal ingredient prepared or the type of cooking performed-vegetable cook, fry cook, or grill cook. Executive chefs and head cooks coordinate the work of the kitchen staff and direct the preparation of meals. They determine serving sizes, plan menus, order food supplies, and oversee kitchen operations to ensure uniform quality and presentation of meals. The terms chef and cook often are used interchangeably, but generally reflect the different types of chefs and the organisational structure of the kitchen staff.

For example, an executive chef is in charge of all food service operations and also may supervise the many kitchens of a hotel, restaurant group, or corporate dining operation. A chef de cuisine reports to an executive chef and is responsible for the daily operations of a single kitchen. A sous chef, or sub chef, is the second-in-command and runs the kitchen in the absence of the chef. Chefs tend to be more highly skilled and better trained than cooks. Many chefs earn fame both for themselves and for their kitchens because of the quality and distinctive nature of the food they serve. The specific responsibilities of most cooks are determined by a number of factors, including the type of restaurant in which they work.

Institution and cafeteria cooks, for example, work in the kitchens of schools, cafeterias, businesses, hospitals, and other institutions. For each meal, they prepare a large quantity of a limited number of entrees, vegetables, and desserts. Restaurant cooks usually prepare a wider selection of dishes, cooking most orders individually. Short-order cooks prepare foods in restaurants and coffee shops that emphasise fast service and quick food preparation. They grill and garnish hamburgers, prepare sandwiches, fry eggs, and cook French fries, often working on several orders at the same time.

Fast-food cooks prepare a limited selection of menu items in fast-food restaurants. They cook and package batches of food, such as hamburgers and fried chicken, to be kept warm until served. Private household cooks plan and prepare meals in private homes according to the client's tastes or dietary needs. They order groceries and supplies, clean the kitchen and wash dishes and utensils. They also may serve meals. Food preparation workers perform routine, repetitive tasks such as readying ingredients for complex dishes, slicing and dicing vegetables, and composing salads and cold items, under the direction of chefs and cooks. They weigh and measure ingredients, go after pots and pans, and stir and strain soups and sauces.

Food preparation workers may cut and grind meats, poultry, and seafood in preparation for cooking. Their responsibilities also include cleaning work areas, equipment, utensils, dishes, and silverware. The number and types of workers employed in kitchens depends on the type of establishment. For example, fast-food establishments offer only a few items, which are prepared by fast-food cooks. Small, full-service restaurants offering casual dining often feature a limited number of easy-to-prepare items supplemented by short-order specialities and ready-made desserts.

Typically, one cook prepares all the food with the help of a short-order cook and one or two other kitchen workers. Grocery and specialty food stores employ chefs, cooks, and food preparation workers to develop recipes and prepare meals to go. Typically, entrees, side dishes, salads, or other items are prepared in large quantities and stored at an appropriate temperature. Servers portion and package items according to customer orders for serving at home.

Working Conditions

Many restaurant and institutional kitchens have modern equipment, convenient work areas, and air conditioning, but kitchens in older and smaller eating places are often not as well designed. Kitchens must be well ventilated, appropriately lit, and properly equipped with sprinkler systems to protect against fires. Kitchen staffs invariably work in small quarters against hot stoves and ovens. They are under constant pressure to prepare meals quickly, while ensuring quality is maintained and safety and sanitation guidelines are observed.

Working conditions vary with the type and quantity of food prepared and the local laws governing food service operations. Workers usually must withstand the pressure and strain of standing for hours at a time, lifting heavy pots and kettles, and working near hot ovens and grills. Job hazards include slips and falls, cuts, and burns, but injuries are seldom serious. Work hours in restaurants may include early mornings, late evenings, holidays, and weekends.

Work schedules of chefs, cooks and other kitchen workers in factory and school cafeterias may be more regular. In 2002, about 33 percent of cooks and 45 percent of food preparation workers had part-time schedules, compared to 16 percent of workers throughout the economy. The wide range in dining hours and the need for fully-staffed kitchens during all open hours creates work opportunities for individuals seeking supplemental income, flexible work hours, or variable schedules.

Chefs, cooks and food preparation workers held nearly 3.0 million jobs in 2002. More than three-fifths of all chefs, cooks, and food preparation workers were employed in restaurants and other food services and drinking places. Nearly one-fifth worked in institutions such as schools, universities, hospitals, and nursing care facilities. Grocery stores, hotels, gasoline stations with convenience stores, and other organisations employed the remainder.

Food Service Managers

Food service managers are responsible for the daily operations of restaurants and other establishments that prepare and serve meals and beverages to customers. Besides coordinating activities among various departments, such as kitchen, dining room, and banquet operations, food service managers ensure that customers are satisfied with their dining experience. In addition, they oversee the inventory and ordering of food, equipment, and supplies and arrange for the routine maintenance and upkeep of the restaurant, its equipment, and facilities. Managers generally are responsible for all of the administrative and human-resource functions of running the business, including recruiting new employees and monitoring employee performance and training.

In most full-service restaurants and institutional food service facilities, the management team consists of a general manager, one or more assistant managers, and an executive chef. The executive chef is responsible for all food preparation activities, including running kitchen operations, planning menus, and maintaining quality standards for food service. In limited-service eating places, such as sandwich shops, coffee bars, or fast-food establishments, managers, not executive chefs, are responsible for supervising routine food preparation operations.

Assistant managers in full-service facilities generally oversee service in the dining rooms and banquet areas. In larger restaurants and fast-food or other food service facilities that serve meals daily and maintain longer hours, individual assistant managers may supervise different shifts of workers. In smaller restaurants, formal titles may be less important, and one person may undertake the work of one or more food service positions. For example, the executive chef also may be the general manager or even sometimes an owner.

One of the most important tasks of food service managers is assisting executive chefs as they select successful menu items. This task varies by establishment depending on the seasonality of menu items, the frequency with which restaurants change their menus, and the introduction of daily or weekly specials. Many restaurants rarely change their menus while others make frequent alterations.

Managers or executive chefs select menu items, taking into account the likely number of customers and the past popularity of dishes. Other issues considered when planning a menu include whether there was any unserved food left over from prior meals that should not be wasted, the need for variety, and the seasonal availability of foods. Managers or executive chefs analyse the recipes of the dishes to determine food, labour, and overhead costs and to assign prices to various dishes. Menus must be developed far enough in advance that supplies can be ordered and received in time.

Managers or executive chefs estimate food needs, place orders with distributors, and schedule the delivery of fresh food and supplies. They plan for routine services or deliveries, such as linen services or the heavy cleaning of dining rooms or kitchen equipment, to occur during slow times or when the dining room is closed. Managers also arrange for equipment maintenance and repairs, and coordinate a variety of services such as waste removal and pest control.

Managers or executive chefs receive deliveries and check the contents against order records. They inspect the quality of fresh meats, poultry, fish, fruits, vegetables, and baked goods to ensure that expectations are met. They meet with representatives from restaurant supply companies and place orders to replenish stocks of tableware, linens, paper products, cleaning supplies, cooking utensils, and furniture and fixtures.

Managers must be good communicators. They need to speak well, often in several languages, with a diverse clientele and staff. They must motivate employees to work as a team, to ensure that food and service meet appropriate standards. Managers also must ensure that written supply orders are clear and unambiguous. Managers interview, hire, train, and, when necessary, fire employees. Retaining good employees is a major challenge facing food service managers.

Managers recruit employees at career fairs, contact schools that offer academic programmes in hospitality or culinary arts, and arrange for newspaper advertising to attract additional applicants. Managers oversee the training of new employees and explain the establishment's policies and practices. They schedule work hours, making sure that enough workers are present to cover each shift. If employees are unable to work, managers may have to call in alternates to cover for them or fill in themselves when needed. Some managers may help with cooking, clearing tables, or other tasks when the restaurant becomes extremely busy.

Food service managers ensure that diners are served properly and in a timely manner. They investigate and resolve customers' complaints about food quality or service. They monitor orders in the kitchen to determine where backups may occur, and they work with the chef to remedy any delays in service. Managers direct the cleaning of the dining areas and the washing of tableware, kitchen utensils, and equipment to comply with company and government sanitation standards.

Managers also monitor the actions of their employees and patrons on a continual basis to ensure the personal safety of everyone. They make sure that health and safety standards and local liquor regulations are obeyed. In addition to their regular duties, food service managers perform a variety of administrative assignments, such as keeping employee work records, preparing the payroll, and completing paperwork to comply with licensing laws and reporting requirements of tax, wage and hour, unemployment compensation, and Social Security laws. Some of this work may be delegated to an assistant manager or bookkeeper, or it may be contracted out, but most general managers retain responsibility for the accuracy of business records.

Managers also maintain records of supply and equipment purchases and ensure that accounts with suppliers are paid. Technology influences the jobs of food service managers in many ways, enhancing efficiency and productivity. Many restaurants use computers to track orders, inventory, and the seating of patrons. Point-of-service (POS) systems allow servers to key in a customer's order, either at the table, using a hand-held device, or from a computer terminal in the dining room, and send the order to the kitchen instantaneously so preparation can begin.

The same system totals and prints checks, functions as a cash register, connects to credit card authorisers, and tracks sales. To minimise food costs and spoilage, many managers use inventory-tracking software to compare the record of sales from the POS with a record of the current inventory. Some establishments enter an inventory of standard ingredients and suppliers into their POS system. When supplies of particular ingredients run low, they can be ordered directly from the supplier using preprogrammed information.

Computers also allow restaurant and food service managers to keep track of employee schedules and paychecks more efficiently. Food service managers use the Internet to track industry news, find recipes, conduct market research, purchase supplies or equipment, recruit employees, and train staff. Internet access also makes service to customers more efficient. Many restaurants maintain Web sites that include menus and online promotions, provide information about the restaurant's location, and offer patrons the option to make a reservation.

Managers tally the cash and charge receipts received and balance them against the record of sales. They are responsible for depositing the day's receipts at the bank or securing them in a safe place. Finally, managers are responsible for locking up the establishment, checking that ovens, grills, and lights are off, and switching on alarm systems.

FOOD-PROCESSING OCCUPATIONS

Food-processing occupations include many different types of workers who process raw food products into the finished goods sold by grocers or wholesalers, restaurants, or institutional food services. These workers perform a variety of tasks and are responsible for producing many of the food products found in every household. Butchers and meat, poultry, and fish cutters and trimmers are employed at different stages in the process by which animal carcasses are converted into manageable pieces of meat, known as boxed meat, that are suitable for sale to wholesalers and retailers.

Meat, poultry, and fish cutters and trimmers commonly work in animal slaughtering and processing plants, while butchers and meatcutters usually are employed at the retail level. As a result, the nature of these jobs varies significantly. In animal slaughtering and processing plants, slaughterers and meatpackers slaughter cattle, hogs, goats, and sheep and cut the carcasses into large wholesale cuts, such as rounds, loins, ribs, and chucks, to facilitate the handling, distribution, and marketing of meat. In some of these plants, slaughterers and meatpackers also further process the large parts into cuts that are ready for retail use. These workers also produce hamburger meat and meat trimmings, which are used to prepare sausages, luncheon meats, and other fabricated meat products.

Slaughterers and meatpackers usually work on assembly lines, with each individual responsible for only a few of the many cuts needed to process a carcass. Depending on the type of cut, they use knives, cleavers, meat saws, bandsaws, or other, often dangerous, equipment. In grocery stores, wholesale establishments that supply meat to restaurants, and institutional food service facilities, butchers and meatcutters separate wholesale cuts of meat into retail cuts or individually sized servings. They cut meat into steaks and chops, shape and tie roasts, and grind beef for sale as chopped meat.

Boneless cuts are prepared with the use of knives, slicers, or power cutters, while bandsaws are required to carve bone-in pieces. Butchers and meatcutters in retail food stores also may weigh, wrap, and label the cuts of meat, arrange them in refrigerated cases for display, and prepare special cuts to fill unique orders. Poultry cutters and trimmers slaughter and cut up chickens, turkeys, and other types of poultry. Although the poultry-processing industry is becoming increasingly automated, many jobs, such as trimming, packing, and deboning, are still done manually.

As in the animal slaughtering and processing industry, most poultry cutters and trimmers perform routine cuts on poultry as it moves along production lines. Unlike some of the other occupations just listed, fish cutters and trimmers, also called fish cleaners, are likely to be employed in both manufacturing and retail establishments. These workers primarily scale, cut, and dress fish by removing the head, scales, and other inedible portions and cutting the fish into steaks or fillets. In retail markets, they may also wait on customers and clean fish to order. Meat, poultry, and fish cutters and trimmers also prepare ready-to-heat foods. This often entails filleting meat or fish or cutting it into bite-sized pieces, preparing and adding vegetables, or applying sauces, marinades, or breading.

Bakers mix and bake ingredients in accordance with recipes to produce varying quantities of breads, pastries, and other baked goods. Bakers commonly are employed in grocery stores and specialty shops and produce small quantities of breads, pastries, and other baked goods for consumption on premises or for sale as specialty baked goods. In manufacturing, bakers produce goods in large quantities, using high-volume mixing machines, ovens, and other equipment.

Goods produced in large quantities usually are available for sale through distributors, grocery stores, or manufacturer's outlets. Others in food-processing occupations include food batchmakers, who set up and operate equipment that mixes, blends, or cooks ingredients used in the manufacture of food products, according to formulas or recipes; food cooking machine operators and tenders, who operate or tend cooking equipment such as steam cooking vats, deep-fry cookers, pressure cookers, kettles, and boilers to prepare food products such as meat, sugar, cheese, and grain; and food and tobacco roasting, baking, and drying machine operators and tenders, who use equipment to reduce the moisture content of food or tobacco products or to process food in preparation for canning. Some of the machines that are used include hearth ovens, kiln driers, roasters, char kilns, steam ovens, and vacuum drying equipment.

Working conditions vary by type and size of establishment. In animal slaughtering and processing plants and large retail food establishments, butchers and meatcutters work in large meatcutting rooms equipped with power machines and conveyors. In small retail markets, the butcher or fish cleaner may work in a cramped space behind the meat or fish counter. To prevent viral and bacterial infections, work areas must be kept clean and sanitary. Butchers and meatcutters, poultry and fish cutters and trimmers, and slaughterer and meatpackers often work in cold, damp rooms, which are refrigerated to prevent meat from spoiling and are damp because meat cutting generates large amounts of blood, condensation, and fat.

Cool, damp floors increase the likelihood of slips and falls. In addition, cool temperatures, long periods of standing, and repetitious physical tasks make the work tiring. As a result, butchers and meat, poultry, and fish cutters are more susceptible to injury than are most other workers. In fact, meatpacking plants had one of the highest incidences of work-related injury and illness of any industry in 2002. Nearly 1 in 7 employees in such plants experienced a work-related injury or illness that year. Injuries include cuts and occasional amputations, which occur when knives, cleavers, or power tools are used improperly. Also, repetitive slicing and lifting often lead to cumulative trauma injuries, such as carpal tunnel syndrome.

To reduce the incidence of cumulative trauma injuries, some employers have reduced employee workloads, added prescribed rest periods, redesigned jobs and tools, and promoted increased awareness of early warning signs so that steps can be taken to prevent further injury. Nevertheless, workers in the occupation still face the serious threat of disabling injuries. Most traditional bakers work in bakeries, cake shops, hot-bread shops, hotels, restaurants, and cafeterias. They also may work in the bakery departments of supermarkets and cruise ships.

Bakers may work under hot and noisy conditions. Also, bakers typically work under strict order deadlines and critical time-sensitive baking requirements, both of which can induce stress. Bakers usually work in shifts and may work early mornings, evenings, weekends, and holidays. While many bakers often work as part of a team, they also may work alone when baking particular items. They may supervise assistants and teach apprentices and trainees. Bakers in retail establishments may be required to serve customers.

Other food-processing workers, such as food batchmakers, food and tobacco roasting, baking, and drying machine operators, and food cooking machine operators and tenders, typically work in production areas that are specially designed for food preservation or processing. Food batchmakers, in particular, work in kitchen-type, assembly-line production facilities. Because this work involves food, work areas must meet governmental sanitary regulations. The ovens, as well as the motors of blenders, mixers, and other equipment, often make work areas very warm and noisy. There are some hazards, such as burns, created by the equipment that these workers use.

Food batchmakers; food and tobacco roasting, baking, and drying machine operators; and food cooking machine operators and tenders spend a great deal of time on their feet and generally work a regular 40-hour week that may include evening and night shifts.

Workers in Food and Beverage Industry

Food and beverage serving and related workers are the front line of customer service in restaurants, coffee shops, and other food service establishments. These workers greet customers, escort them to seats and hand them menus, take food and drink orders, and serve food and beverages. They also answer questions, explain menu items and specials, and keep tables and dining areas clean and set for new diners.

Most work as part of a team, helping coworkers during busy times to improve workflow and customer service. Waiters and waitresses, the largest group of these workers, take customers' orders, serve food and beverages, prepare itemised checks, and sometimes accept payment.

Their specific duties vary considerably, depending on the establishment. In coffee shops serving routine, straightforward fare, such as salads, soups, and sandwiches, servers are expected to provide fast, efficient, and courteous service.

In fine dining restaurants, where more complicated meals are prepared and often served over several courses, waiters and waitresses provide more formal service emphasising personal, attentive treatment and a more leisurely pace. They may recommend certain dishes and identify ingredients or explain how various items on the menu are prepared. Some prepare salads, desserts, or other menu items tableside. Additionally, they may check the identification of patrons to ensure they meet the minimum age requirement for the purchase of alcohol and tobacco products. Waiters and waitresses sometimes perform the duties of other food and beverage service workers.

These tasks may include escorting guests to tables, serving customers seated at counters, clearing and setting up tables, or operating a cash register. However, full-service restaurants frequently hire other staff, such as hosts and hostesses, cashiers, or dining room attendants, to perform these duties. Bartenders fill drink orders either taken directly from patrons at the bar or through waiters and waitresses who place drink orders for dining room customers. Bartenders check identification of customers seated at the bar, to ensure they meet the minimum age requirement for the purchase of alcohol and tobacco products. They prepare mixed drinks, serve bottled or draught beer, and pour wine or other beverages.

Bartenders must know a wide range of drink recipes and be able to mix drinks accurately, quickly, and without waste. Besides mixing and serving drinks, bartenders stock and prepare garnishes for drinks; maintain an adequate supply of ice, glasses, and other bar supplies; and keep the bar area clean for customers. They also may collect payment, operate the cash register, wash glassware and utensils, and serve food to customers seated at the bar.

Bartenders usually are responsible for ordering and maintaining an inventory of liquor, mixes, and other bar supplies. The majority of bartenders directly serve and interact with patrons. Bartenders should be friendly and enjoy mingling with customers. Bartenders at service bars, on the other hand, have less contact with customers. They work in small bars often located off the kitchen in restaurants, hotels, and clubs where only waiters and waitresses place drink orders.

Some establishments, especially larger, higher volume ones, use equipment that automatically pours and mixes drinks at the push of a button. Bartenders who use this equipment, however, still must work quickly to handle a large volume of drink orders and be familiar with the ingredients for special drink requests. Much of a bartender's work still must be done by hand to fill each individual order. Hosts and hostesses welcome guests and maintain reservation or waiting lists. They may direct patrons to coatrooms, restrooms, or to a place to wait until their table is ready.

Hosts and hostesses assign guests to tables suitable for the size of their group, escort patrons to their seats, and provide menus. They also schedule dining reservations, arrange parties, and organise any special services that are required. In some restaurants, they act as cashiers. Dining room and cafeteria attendants and bartender helpers assist waiters, waitresses, and bartenders by cleaning tables, removing dirty dishes, and keeping serving areas stocked with supplies.

Sometimes called backwaiters or runners, they bring meals out of the kitchen and assist waiters and waitresses by distributing dishes to individual diners. They also replenish the supply of clean linens, dishes, silverware, and glasses in the dining room and keep the bar stocked with glasses, liquor, ice, and drink garnishes. Dining room attendants set tables with clean tablecloths, napkins, silverware, glasses, and dishes and serve ice water, rolls, and butter. At the conclusion of meals, they remove dirty dishes and soiled linens from tables.

Cafeteria attendants stock serving tables with food, trays, dishes, and silverware and may carry trays to dining tables for patrons. Bartender helpers keep bar equipment clean and wash glasses. Dishwashers clean dishes, cutlery, and kitchen utensils and equipment. Counter attendants take orders and serve food in cafeterias, coffee shops, and carryout eateries. In cafeterias, they serve food displayed on steam tables, carve meat, dish out vegetables, ladle sauces and soups, and fill beverage glasses.

In lunchrooms and coffee shops, counter attendants take orders from customers seated at the counter, transmit orders to the kitchen, and pick up and serve food. They also fill cups with coffee, soda, and other beverages and prepare fountain specialities, such as milkshakes and ice cream sundaes. Counter attendants also take carryout orders from diners and wrap or place items in containers. They clean counters, write itemised checks, and sometimes accept payment. Some counter attendants may prepare short-order items, such as sandwiches and salads.

Some food and beverage serving workers take orders from customers at counters or drive-through windows at fast-food restaurants. They assemble orders, hand them to customers, and accept payment. Many of these are combined food preparation and serving workers who also cook and package food, make coffee, and fill beverage cups using drink-dispensing machines.

Other workers serve food to patrons outside of a restaurant environment, such as in hotels, hospital rooms, or cars. Food and beverage service workers are on their feet most of the time and often carry heavy trays of food, dishes, and glassware. During busy dining periods, they are under pressure to serve customers quickly and efficiently. The work is relatively safe, but care must be taken to avoid slips, falls, and burns. Part-time work is more common among food and beverage serving and related workers than among workers in almost any other occupation.

Food service and drinking establishments typically maintain long dining hours and offer flexible and varied work opportunities. Many food and beverage serving and related workers work evenings, weekends, and holidays. Some work split shifts-they work for several hours during the middle of the day, take a few hours off in the afternoon, and then return to their jobs for evening hours. Many students and teenagers seek part time or seasonal work as food and beverage serving and related workers as a first job to gain work experience or to earn spending money while in school. Around one-fourth of food and beverage serving and related workers were 16 to 19 years old-about 5 times the proportion for all workers.

The overwhelming majority of jobs for food and beverage serving and related workers were found in food services and drinking places, such as restaurants, coffee shops, and bars. Other jobs were found primarily in traveller accommodation (hotels); amusement, gambling, and recreation industries; educational services; grocery stores; nursing care facilities; civic and social organisations; and hospitals. Jobs are located throughout the country but are typically plentiful in large cities and tourist areas. Vacation resorts offer seasonal employment, and some workers alternate between summer and winter resorts, instead of remaining in one area the entire year.

There are no specific educational requirements for food and beverage service jobs. Many employers prefer to hire high school graduates for waiter and waitress, bartender, and host and hostess positions, but completion of high school usually is not required for fast-food workers, counter attendants, dishwashers, and dining room attendants and bartender helpers. A job as a food and beverage service worker serves as a source of immediate income, rather than a career, for many people.

Many entrants to these jobs are in their late teens or early twenties and have a high school education or less. Usually, they have little or no work experience. Many are full-time students or homemakers. Food and beverage service jobs are a major source of part-time employment for high school and college students. Restaurants rely on good food and quality customer service to retain loyal customers and succeed in a competitive industry.

Food and beverage serving and related workers who exhibit excellent personal qualities, such as a neat clean appearance, a well-spoken manner, an ability to work as a member of team, and a pleasant way with patrons, will be highly sought after. Waiters and waitresses need a good memory to avoid confusing customers' orders and to recall faces, names, and preferences of frequent patrons. These workers also should be comfortable using computers to place orders and generate customers' bills.

Some may need to be quick at arithmetic so they can total bills manually. Knowledge of a foreign language is helpful to communicate with a diverse clientele and staff. Prior experience waiting on tables is preferred by restaurants and hotels that have rigid table service standards. Jobs at these establishments often offer higher wages and have greater income potential from tips, but they may also have stiffer employment requirements, such as higher education or training standards, than other establishments. Usually, bartenders must be at least 21 years of age, but employers prefer to hire people who are 25 or older.

Bartenders should be familiar with State and local laws concerning the sale of alcoholic beverages. Most food and beverage serving and related workers pick up their skills on the job by observing and working with more experienced workers. Some employers, particularly those in fast-food restaurants, use self-instruction programmes with audiovisual presentations and instructional booklets to teach new employees food preparation and service skills. Some public and private vocational schools, restaurant associations, and large restaurant chains provide classroom training in a generalised food service curriculum.

Some bartenders acquire their skills by attending a bartending or vocational and technical school. These programmes often include instruction on State and local laws and regulations, cocktail recipes, attire and conduct, and stocking a bar. Some of these schools help their graduates find jobs. Although few employers require any minimum level of educational attainment, some specialised training is usually needed in food handling and legal issues surrounding serving alcoholic beverages and tobacco.

Employers are more likely to hire and promote based on people skills and personal qualities rather than education. Due to the relatively small size of most food-serving establishments, opportunities for promotion are limited. After gaining experience, some dining room and cafeteria attendants and bartender helpers advance to waiter, waitress, or bartender jobs. For waiters, waitresses, and bartenders, advancement usually is limited to finding a job in a busier or more expensive restaurant or bar where prospects for tip earnings are better.

A few bartenders open their own businesses. Some hosts and hostesses and waiters and waitresses advance to supervisory jobs, such as maitre d'hotel, dining room supervisor, or restaurant manager. In larger restaurant chains, food and beverage service workers who excel at their work often are invited to enter the company's formal management training programme. Job openings are expected to be abundant for food and beverage serving and related workers.

While employment growth will account for many new jobs, the overwhelming majority of openings will arise from the need to replace the high proportion of workers who leave the occupations each year. There is substantial movement into and out of these occupations because education and training requirements are minimal, and the predominance of part-time jobs is attractive to people seeking a short-term source of income rather than a career. However, keen competition is expected for bartender, waiter and waitress, and other food and beverage service jobs in popular restaurants and fine dining establishments, where potential earnings from tips are greatest.

13

Food Preservation

Food preservation is the process of treating and handling food in such a way as to stop or greatly slow down spoilage to prevent foodborne illness while maintaining nutritional value, texture and flavour.

Methods for Preservation

Common methods of applying these processes include drying, freeze drying, freezing, vacuum-packing, canning, preserving in syrup, sugar crystalisation, food irradiation, adding preservatives or inert gases such as Carbon dioxide. Other methods that not only help to preserve food, but also add flavour, include pickling, salting, smoking, preserving in syrup or alcohol, sugar crystalisation and curing.

Drying

One of the oldest method of food preservation is by drying, which reduces water activity sufficient to delay or prevent bacterial growth. Most types of meat can be dried and this is especially valuable in the case of pig meat since this is difficult to keep without preservation. Many fruits can also be dried and the process is often applied to apples, pears, bananas, mangos, papaya, coconut etc. Currants, Sultanas and Raisins are all form of dried Grapes. Drying is also the normal means of preservation for cereal grains such as wheat, maize, oats, barley, rice, millet and rye. Drying removes enough moisture from the food so bacteria, yeasts and molds can't grow.

Drying also slows down the action of enzymes because it removes moisture, the food shrinks, and it becomes lighter in weight. When food is ready for use, add water. Dry foods in the oven or a food dehydrator by using the right combination of warmth, low humidity and air currents. Sun drying is not recommended in Minnesota due to high humidity and cool night temperatures. In drying, a warm temperature allows the moisture to evaporate. Air currents speed up drying. Low humidity allows moisture to move from the food to the air.

Drying food is a slow process. In a dehydrator, it takes six or more hours to dry foods. In the oven, it takes eight or more hours. Drying time depends on the type of food, the thickness of the cut, the moisture content of the food and the drying method. Don't speed up the drying time by turning up the oven. You will cook the food on the outside before it dries on the inside. This is called "case hardening." The food may appear dry on the outside but is wet on the inside. It will mold later on in storage.

Vegetables are dry when they are brittle, fruits when they feel like leather. After foods are dried, allow 30 minutes to one hour cooling time. Too long a cooling period allows moisture from the air to re-enter the food. Proper storage prevents insects and rodents from eating the food. It also keeps moisture out and saves nutrients. Use glass jars, metal cans or boxes with tight-fitting lids or vapour-proof freezer cartons. Heavy-duty plastic bags with press-together seals are acceptable, but are not insect-

or rodent-proof. Screw lids or covers on glass jars to prevent insect contamination, but it is not necessary to heat-process the jars.

Dried foods keep four months to one year depending on storage conditions. Store in cool, dry, dark areas. For best quality, store under 60 degrees Fahrenheit. Although it is not necessary to store dried food in a refrigerator or freezer, except for meat jerky, low temperatures extend the shelf life. Check containers within seven to 10 days to see if moisture is present. If you see moisture, remove food and redry at 140 to 160 degrees Fahrenheit. If food is moldy, discard it, throw away the plastic freezer bag or sterilise the jar.

Dried fruits can be eaten as nutritious snacks, or can be soaked in water or juice for one to two hours and used in favourite recipes. Sliced vegetables can be eaten dried as tasty vegetable chips for dips. Most vegetables are refreshed with water before use. The water can be added back to vegetables by soaking in tap water for one to two hours. Use two cups of water for each cup of dried food. Using boiling water speeds up the soaking period. Dried vegetables can be added directly to soups or stews without pre-soaking, drawing on the liquid in the soup or stew for rehydration during cooking.

Drying preserves food by lowering the amount of water or moisture in the food material. This is necessary to prevent microbial growth and chemical reactions which can only occur when enough water is present in the food. Equilibrium Relative Humidity (ERH) is a term used to describe the availability of the water to the chemical environment and microorganisms present in foods. The equilibrium relative humidity or percent ERH scale varies from zero to 100.

If a food of a certain moisture content is put in a closed chamber which is set to some relative humidity, the food will change its moisture content in an attempt to equal the ERH of the chamber. If a dry food such as a cracker which has an ERH equal to 11 percent is placed in a chamber with a high ERH, for example 60 percent, the cracker will gain water from the air until it reaches the ERH of the air, in this case the cracker will lose its crispness.

If a fresh tissue food such as lettuce which has an ERH equal to 98 percent is placed in a chamber set at 60 percent ERH, the lettuce will lose moisture to the air and become wilted. These two foods will have different moistures at 60 percent ERH, but they will both have the same availability of water to chemical reactions and microorganisms present in the food. Fresh tissue foods, such as meat, vegetables, and fruit products, have an ERH close to 100 percent. An ERH level this high means that the water present in these foods is available for rapid growth of microorganisms leading to deterioration and spoilage of the food.

By drying foods it is possible to lower the percent ERH. As the percent ERH is lowered, the growth of microorganisms slows or ceases since the water is no longer as available for their growth. This occurs at an ERH of 60 percent. Therefore, all foods must be dried to below 60 percent ERH and kept in a dry environment to be shelf stable from microbial growth because microorganisms cannot survive below this ERH level.

Dehydration

Sun-drying: Sun-drying requires constant exposure to direct sunlight during the day and a relative humidity of less than 20 percent. Foods dried in the sun can take from 3-4 days to dry and if the humidity is high, as is generally the case in Minnesota, the food will mold before it dries.

The sun-drying process is inefficient because it requires much more space and drying time than drying in conventional home driers. In addition, food dried in the sun is exposed to dirt, insects, rodents, and bird wastes. The practice of sun-drying is not recommended for home food preservation because complete drying cannot be assured and the quality of the food is questionable.

Dehydrators: Purchased home food dehydrators and portable convection ovens fitted with drying trays, provide better control over climatic conditions and food quality than sun-drying. Drying foods in a conventional oven gives much less satisfactory results. Home dehydrators and convection ovens are equipped with a heating element and fan which blows hot, dry air at moderate speeds around the food. The air serves two purposes. It supplies the heat needed to evaporate the water. As the air heats up its relative humidity decreases allowing the food to dry at a faster rate and reach a low equilibrium relative humidity. The dry air blown across the food also serves to carry away the water vapour.

The air must be kept in motion by the fan because stagnant air takes on as much moisture as it can hold, and if it is not removed, drying no longer takes place. Both counter top dehydrators and portable convection ovens can be used on a 110/120 volt general purpose circuit (15 AMP). The food dehydrators draw 525-800 watts; the convection ovens draw about 1500 watts and should not be used on the same general household circuit with other heating appliances such as a coffee maker or toaster. This may be an important consideration in view of the fact that convection ovens used for drying may be running for many hours.

Food dehydrators and convection ovens differ in their range of temperature settings and available square feet of drying space. The range of temperature settings for dehydrators as a low of 85° to 110° F up to a high of 140° to 145° F. The range for convection ovens has a low of 140° to 175° F up to a high of 500° F. Food dehydrators are usually made to handle more racks and, therefore, have more square feet of drying space than portable convection ovens. The appliances require 18-24 inches of counter space and vary in height from 10-16 inches. The height is a consideration if it is to fit on a counter with cabinets above. Food dehydrators range in cost from $100 to $250; convection ovens that recommend drying range from $150 to $200; drying racks for convection ovens would be $25 to $50 extra.

Storage problems

Dried foods must be stored properly to maintain the low moisture content and to prevent microbial deterioration. Before packing foods, the dried pieces should be allowed to cool for a short amount of time. Immediately after the product has cooled the food should be stored. To store dried foods, place the dried food in plastic bags, press out air, seal or close, and then place in glass jars which are tightly sealed. Plastic containers or metal cans with plastic lids are not recommended because moisture can enter through the container.

To be sure that the food remains dry, add dessicant or silica gel which you can purchase in the notions or housewares section of a department store or at hobby shops. Place the substance in the glass jar to cover the bottom of the container to a depth of ¼-inch thick. The dessicant absorbs any moisture from the surroundings and prevents the food from absorbing moisture. Place the dried food wrapped in a sealed plastic bag over the dessicant and tightly seal the jar. Packaged dried food should be stored in a dry, cool, 60° F place.

Dried food should also be kept out of the sun to prevent discoloration and nutrient loss. Dried foods in sealed plastic bags may also be stored in the refrigerator or freezer. In general, the shelf life of home dried vegetables and fruits stored at 60° F is 4 to 6 months. If the product is stored at 70° F, shelf life will be shortened. The shelf life of food dried in the home is not as long as the shelf life of commercially freeze-dried products. This is because freeze-dried foods are first frozen at -40° F and then placed in a chamber connected to a vacuum pump.

Heat is applied to the frozen food after the air is evacuated from the chamber and the ice sublimes or evaporates directly into vapour. Because the food is frozen and is at a low temperature during drying, there is little nutrient loss and textural damage. Freeze-drying is not practical for home use because elaborate and expensive equipment is necessary.

Instructions for Drying

All foods should be prepared by properly sorting, washing, and peeling. If possible, gather vegetables or fruits early in the morning and start the drying process as soon as possible to prevent browning or wilting.

Vegetables

Vegetables must be blanched to inactivate enzymes. The blanching time is counted as soon as the vegetable is immersed in vigorously boiling water. Do not add so much food that the water stops boiling. The quality of water used to blanch the vegetables can have an effect on the texture of certain vegetables. Very hard water can cause the toughening of vegetables, such as green beans. If you have problems with excessively tough green beans, check into the level of hardness in your water supply.

1. *To Blanch in Boiling Water*
   - — Use 1 gallon water for each pound of vegetable.
   - — Bring water to rolling boil.

— Immerse wire basket or mesh bag containing vegetable.

— Cover kettle and boil at top heat the required length of time.

— Begin counting time as you place the vegetable in water. You may use the same blanching water 2 or 3 times. Keep it at required level. Change the water if it becomes cloudy.

— Drain the vegetables thoroughly.

2. *To Blanch in Steam*

— Put 1 inch of water in kettle, bring to a rolling boil.

— Suspend a thin layer of vegetables in steaming basket or loose cheese cloth bag over rapidly boiling water.

— Cover and steam blanch vegetables required amount of time as listed on table.

— Remove from steamer.

Fruits

Sodium Bisulphite: Pretreating fruit with sodium bisulfite will reduce vitamin loss, flavour loss, browning, and deterioration during storage. Sodium sulphite and sodium metabisulphite, available at wine-making shops, may also be used. However, sulphite-sensitive individuals should not use this method. Prepare a solution of 1 tablespoon sodium bisulfite, or 2 tablespoons sodium sulphite, or 4 tablespoons of sodium metabisulfite to a gallon of water. Soak slices of fruit for 5 minutes and halves of fruit for 15 minutes. When soaking is complete, remove fruit and rinse lightly under cold tap water. Then place the fruit on the drying trays.

Ascorbic Acid: Ascorbic acid (vitamin C) mixed with water is a safe way to prevent fruit browning. However, its protection does not last as long as sulphiting. Ascorbic acid is available in the powdered or tablet form, from drugstores or grocery stores. One teaspoon of powdered ascorbic acid is equal to 3000 mg of ascorbic acid in tablet form.

Directions for Use: Mix 1 teaspoon of powdered ascorbic acid (or 3000 mg of ascorbic acid tablets, crushed) in 2 cups water. Place the fruit in the solution for 3 to 5 minutes. Remove fruit, drain well and place on dryer trays. After this solution is used twice, add more acid.

Fruit Juice Dip: A fruit juice that is high in vitamin C can also be used as a pretreatment, though it is not as effective as pure ascorbic acid. Juices high in vitamin C include orange, lemon, pineapple, grape and cranberry. Each juice adds its own colour and flavour to the fruit.

Directions for Use: Place enough juice to cover fruit in a bowl. Add cut fruit. Soak 3 to 5 minutes, remove fruit, drain well and place on dryer trays. This solution may be used twice, before being replaced.

Fruit Leathers: These are chewy candy-like products which are made by pureeing fresh fruits in a blender or food processor. The thick pureed fruit is poured onto a dehydrator tray lined with 4 mil food grade plastic and dried. The puree layer should not be more than ¼-inch thick. Leave a 1 inch border around the puree to allow for spreading during drying. It usually takes 6 to 8 hours to dry fruit leathers.

Dried vegetables need about 2 hours soaking time before cooking. When you soak or rehydrate the vegetables they should plump to nearly the same size they were when fresh. Start with 1½ to 2 cups of water for each cup of dried vegetables. If necessary, add more water during the soaking process. Cook the vegetables in the same water in which they have soaked to save nutrients. Boil or simmer dried vegetables in soups, stews, or other dishes cooked in liquid. Most dried fruit can be eaten or used in recipes as it is. If you wish to plump or soften the fruit slightly to make it more chewable, you can use one of these methods:

— Cover the dried fruit with boiling water. Let it stand for 5 minutes then drain.

— Place the dried fruit in the top of a steamer over boiling water and steam 3 to 5 minutes until the fruit is plump.

Eggs, fish, poultry, and meat (except beef jerky) are not recommended for home drying. Salmonella and Staphylococcus bacteria, which thrive on these foods, can survive and grow at low temperatures used to dry meat and dairy products. These bacteria grow very rapidly in meat and poultry products because all the nutrient needs of these pathogenic or disease producing bacteria are supplied by meats, eggs, and dairy products.

The growth of the pathogenic bacteria will stop when 60 percent ERH is reached, but when water is added to the product, the bacteria will grow again. The poisonous toxin produced by Staphylococcus is not destroyed by cooking the food. Salmonella and Staphylococcus have caused food poisoning outbreaks in home-dried foods.

Freeze Drying

Frozen food is subjected to very low air pressures which cause the water content to evaporate without passing through the water stage. This produces a very low water content food without addition of cooking flavours or presence of denatured proteins. Freeze drying is commonly used to preserve small vegetables such as peas and beans and also a wide range of ready-made foods, such as soups and other convenience foods which only require the addition of hot water prior to consumption. Many foods intended for campers and hikers are freeze dried because of the considerable weight advantage over non freeze dried items. Freeze drying is also widely used for preparation of dried milk and whey products.

Freezing

Probably as old as drying, many Arctic communities would preserve food in holes or larders dug into the ice. There is a tradition in Scandinavia of preserving fish and especially herrings in this way. The addition of urine at the time of packing the fish into the ice is said to assist in preservation and to improve the flavour of the food when eaten. Freezing is also one of the most commonly used processes commercially and domestically for preserving a very wide range of food stuffs including prepared footstuffs which would not have required freezing in their unprepared state. I.e. Potato waffles are stores in the freezer but potatoes themselves require only a cool dark place to ensure many months' storage. Cold stores provide large volume, long term storage for strategic food stocks held in case of national emergency in many countries.

Every year, thousands of callers to the USDA Meat and Poultry Hotline aren't sure about the safety of items stored in their own home freezers. The confusion seems to be based on the fact that few people understand how freezing protects food. Some foods simply don't freeze well. Examples are mayonnaise, cream sauce and lettuce. Raw meat and poultry maintain their quality longer than their cooked counterparts because moisture is lost during cooking.

Food stored constantly at 0°F will always be safe. Only the quality suffers with lengthy freezer storage. Freezing keeps food safe by slowing the movement of molecules, causing microbes to enter a dormant stage. Freezing preserves food for extended periods because it prevents the growth of microorganisms that cause both food spoilage and foodborne illness.

Freezing to 0°F inactivates any microbes—bacteria, yeasts and molds—present in food. Once thawed, however, these microbes can again become active, multiplying under the right conditions to levels that can lead to foodborne illness. Since they will then grow at about the same rate as microorganisms on fresh food, you must handle thawed items as you would any perishable food.

Trichina and other parasites can be destroyed by sub-zero freezing temperatures. However, very strict government-supervised conditions must be met. It is not recommended to rely on home freezing to destroy trichina. Thorough cooking will destroy all parasites.

Freshness and quality at the time of freezing affect the condition of frozen foods. If frozen at peak quality, foods emerge tasting better than foods frozen near the end of their useful life. So freeze items you won't use quickly sooner rather than later. Store all foods at 0° F or lower to retain vitamin content, colour, flavour and texture.

The freezing process itself does not destroy nutrients. In meat and poultry products, there is little change in nutrient value during freezer storage. Enzyme activity can lead to the deterioration of food quality. Enzymes present in animals, vegetables and fruit promote chemical reactions, such as ripening. Freezing only slows the enzyme activity that takes place in foods. It does not halt these reactions which continue after harvesting.

Enzyme activity does not harm frozen meats or fish and is neutralised by the acids in frozen fruits. But most vegetables that freeze well are low acid and require a brief, partial cooking to prevent deterioration. This is called "blanching." For successful freezing, blanch or partially cook vegetables in boiling water or in a microwave oven. Then rapidly chill the vegetables prior to freezing and storage.

Proper packaging helps maintain quality and prevent "freezer burn." It is safe to freeze meat or poultry directly in its supermarket wrapping but this type of wrap is permeable to air. Unless you will be using the food in a month or two, overwrap these packages as you would any food for long-term storage using airtight heavy-duty foil, (freezer) plastic wrap or freezer paper, or place the package inside a (freezer) plastic bag. Use these materials or airtight freezer containers to repackage family packs into smaller amounts. It is not necessary to rinse meat and poultry before freezing. Freeze unopened vacuum packages as is. If you notice that a package has accidentally been torn or has opened while food is in the freezer, the food is still safe to use; merely overwrap or rewrap it.

Freezer burn does not make food unsafe, merely dry in spots. It appears as grayish-brown leathery spots and is caused by air reaching the surface of the food. Cut freezer-burned portions away either before or after cooking the food. Heavily freezer-burned foods may have to be discarded for quality reasons.

The bright red colour of meat as purchased usually turns dark or pale brown depending on its variety. This may be due to lack of oxygen, freezer burn or abnormally long storage. Freezing doesn't usually cause colour changes in poultry. However, the bones and the meat near them can become dark. Bone darkening results when pigment seeps through the porous bones of young poultry into the surrounding tissues when the poultry meat is frozen and thawed. The dulling of colour in frozen vegetables and cooked foods is usually the result of excessive drying due to improper packaging or over-lengthy storage. Freeze food as fast as possible to maintain its quality.

Rapid freezing prevents undesirable large ice crystals from forming throughout the product because the molecules don't have time to take their positions in the characteristic six-sided snowflake. Slow freezing creates large, disruptive ice crystals. During thawing, they damage the cells and dissolve emulsions. This causes meat to "drip"—lose juiciness. Emulsions such as mayonnaise or cream will separate and appear curdled. Ideally, a food 2-inches thick should freeze completely in about 2 hours. If your home freezer has a "quick-freeze" shelf, use it. Never stack packages to be frozen. Instead, spread them out in one layer on various shelves, stacking them only after frozen solid.

Vacuum Packing

Vacuum-packing stores food in a vacuum environment, usually in an air-tight bag or bottle. The vacuum environment strips bacteria of oxygen needed for survival, hence preventing the food from spoiling. Vacuum-packing is commonly used for storing nuts.

Canning

Canning involves cooking fruits or vegetables, sealing them in sterile cans or jars, and boiling the containers to kill or weaken any remaining bacteria. Various foods have varying degrees of natural protection against spoilage and may require that the final step occur in a pressure cooker. High-acid fruits like strawberries require no preservatives to can and only a short boiling cycle, whereas marginal fruits such as tomatoes require longer boiling and addition of other acidic elements. Many vegetables require pressure canning. Food preserved by canning or bottling is at immediate risk of spoilage once the can or bottle has been opened.

To can means to heat process food in a glass jar with a lid in place. Heat processing kills microorganisms—bacteria, yeast, and mold—that contaminate food and cause food spoilage and/or foodborne illness. Processing can be done in a water bath canner or a pressure canner, depending on the food's acidity. High-acid foods (all fruits except figs that are not acidified) can be safely processed in a water bath canner. Acidified figs and tomatoes can also be safely processed in a water bath canner. Microorganisms in or on high-acid foods are easily killed at 212F (the temperature of boiling water). Low-acid foods (vegetables and tomatoes that are not acidified) must be processed in a pressure canner.

The bacteria that produces botulinum toxin cannot grow in high-acid foods but can grow in low-acid foods. The bacteria, Clostridium botulinum, have spores that survive for hours in boiling water. However, these spores are destroyed within a reasonable amount of time at 240F (the temperature reached inside a weighted gauge pressure canner at 10 pounds pressure and at 11 pounds pressure inside a dial-gauge canner). If low-acid food is processed in a water bath canner, botulinum spores on the food will survive. In the absence of air, a condition found inside a jar after processing, the spores become living bacteria. As the bacteria grow, they form toxins.

Eating even a drop of this potent toxin can be fatal to humans and animals. Many cases of botulism have been associated with eating low-acid foods that were improperly canned at home. To make sure your home canned foods are safe, carefully follow the canning instructions in this fact sheet. Process high-acid foods in a water bath canner and low-acid foods in a pressure canner. Never process any foods in a conventional oven, microwave oven, steamer or dishwasher, as these methods do not kill microorganisms that cause food spoilage and/or foodborne illness.

Select high quality, unblemished fruits and vegetables for canning. Canning will not improve quality. Can them as soon as possible after harvesting. If you must store fruits and vegetables before canning, keep them in the refrigerator. If you buy fruits or vegetables to can, get them fresh from a local farmer's market, a roadside stand or a pick- your-own farm. Thoroughly wash fruits and vegetables before canning even if they will be peeled. Garden soil contains bacteria.

Wash by scrubbing with a vegetable brush and rinsing thoroughly. Or, if more practical, soak in water for several minutes. Lift out of the water so the soil that has been washed off won't settle back on the food. Peel, pit, and/or slice only as much food as you can process at one time. Some fruits and vegetables (apples, apricots, nectarines, peaches, pears and potatoes) darken when cut. To prevent darkening, keep raw, prepared produce in a solution of one teaspoon ascorbic acid to one gallon of cold water. Check among the canners' supplies in the supermarket to get this product.

Sugar and salt

Sugar helps retain the colour, shape, and texture of canned fruits. Sugar is usually added as a syrup. To make syrup, pour 4 cups of water into a saucepan and add: 2 cups of sugar to make 5 cups of light syrup or 3 cups of sugar to make 5 1/2 cups of medium syrup or 4 1/4 cups of sugar to make 6 1/2 cups of heavy syrup. Heat until the sugar dissolves. Make 1 to 1-1/2 cups of syrup for each quart of fruit. Up to half the sugar used in making syrup can be replaced with light corn syrup or mild-flavoured honey.

Fruits also can be safely canned without sugar. Pack the fruit in extracted juice, in juice from another fruit (such as bottled apple juice, pineapple juice, or white grape juice) or in water. Salt may be added to vegetables and tomatoes before canning. Because its only function is flavour, it can safely be omitted. Canning fruits and vegetables without adding sugar or salt does not affect processing times or microbiological safety.

Boiling water canners

Most boiling water canners are made of aluminum or porcelain-covered steel. They have fitted lids and removable racks that are either perforated or shaped wire racks. The canner must be deep enough so that at least one inch of briskly boiling water will be over the tops of jars during processing. Some boiling water canners do not have completely flat bottoms. A flat bottom must be used on an electric range. Either a flat or ridged bottom may be used on a gas burner. To ensure uniform processing of all jars with an electric range, the canner should be no more than 4 inches wider in diameter than the element on which it is heated.

Pressure canners

Pressure canners for use in the home were extensively redesigned beginning in the 1970's. Models made before the 1970's were heavy-walled kettles with clamp-on or turn-on lids. They were fitted with a dial gauge, a vent port in the form of a petcock or covered with a counterweight, and a safety fuse. Modern pressure canners are lightweight, thin-walled kettles; most have turn-on lids fitted with gaskets. They all have removable racks, an automatic vent/cover lock, a vent port (steam vent), and a safety fuse.

Today's pressure canner may have a dial gauge for indicating the pressure or a weighted gauge, for indicating and regulating the pressure. Pressure canners come deep enough for one layer of quart or smaller size jars, or deep enough for two layers of pint or smaller size jars.

Smoking

Smoking is sometimes done in conjunction with drying. Although not sufficient by itself to permit long term storage of food, smoking adds chemicals, particularly poly aromatic hydrocarbons (PAHs) that help inhibit the growth of micro-organisms.

Curing

Curing draws moisture from the meat through a process of osmosis. Meat is cured with salt or sugar, or a combination of the two. Nitrates and nitrites are also often used to cure meat.

Sugar

Sugar is used to preserve fruits, either in syrup with fruit such as apples, pears, peaches, apricots, plums or in crystalised form where the preserved material is cooked in sugar to the point of crystralisation and the resultant product is then stored dry. This method is used for the skins of citrus fruit (candied peel)), angelica and ginger. A modification of this process produces glacé fruit such as glacé cherries where the fruit is preserved in sugar but is then extracted from the syrup and sold, the preservation being maintained by the sugar content of the fruit and the superficial coating of syrup. The use of sugar is often combined with alcohol for preservation of luxury products such as fruit in Brandy or other sprits. These should not be confused with fruit flavoured spirits such as Cherry Brandy or Sloe gin

Pickling

Pickling is a method of preserving food by placing it or cooking it in a substance that inhibits or kills bacteria and other micro-organisms, This material must also be fit for human consumption. Typical pickling agents include brine (high in salt), vinegar, ethanol and vegetable oil especially olive oil but also many other oils. Most pickling processes also involve heating or boiling so that the food being preserved becomes saturated with the pickling agent. A less-common form of pickling uses sodium hydroxide (lye) to make the food too alkaline for bacterial growth. Lye will saponify fats in the food, which will change its flavour and texture. Lutefisk uses lye in its preparation, as do some olive recipes.

Jellying

Food may be preserved by cooking in a material that solidifies to form a gel. Such materials include gelatine, agar, maize flour and arrowroot flour. Some foods naturally form a protein gel when cooked such as Eels and elvers, and Sipunculid worms which are a delicacy in the town of Xiamen in Fujian province of China. Jellied eels are a delicacy in the East End of London where they are eaten with mashed potatoes. Potted meats in aspic, (the gel made from arrowroot flour) were a common way of serving meat off-cuts in the UK until the 1950s

Irradiation

A 1950s issue of Popular Mechanics details the impending arrival of "food irradiation". However, at the present time, the implications surrounding the irradiation of food are still not fully understood, and the technology is therefore still not in widespread use. However, irradiation of potatoes, strawberries, and meat is common in many countries where refrigerated facilities and trucks are not common. In 2002, the FDA permitted irradiation of meat and poultry to reduce the spread of E. coli and salmonella. In the US and most of Europe irradiation of spices is common, as the only alternative (treatment with gas) has been shown to be potentially carcinogenic. The process is called "cold pasteurisation" to avoid the reduced sales from negative implications of the term "irradiation".

Modified Atmosphere

Modified atmosphere is a way to preserve food operating on the atmosphere around it. Salad crops which are notoriously difficult to preserve are now being packaged in sealed bags with an atmosphere modified to reduce the oxygen concentration and increase the carbon dioxide concentration. There is concern that although salad vegetables retain their appearance and texture in such conditions, this method of preservation may not retain nutrient content, especially vitamins. Grains may be preserved using carbon dioxide. A block of dry ice is placed in the bottom and the can is filled with grain. The can is then "burped" of excess gas. The carbon dioxide from the sublimation of the dry ice prevents insects, mold, and oxidation from damaging the grain. Grain stored in this way can survive five years in a moist garage.

Clamps

Many root vegetables are very resistant to spoilage and require no other preservation other than storage in cool dark conditions, usually in field clamps.

Biological Processes

Some foods, such as many traditional cheeses, will keep for a long time without use of any special procedures. The preservation occurs because of the presence in very high numbers of beneficial bacteria or fungi which use their own biological defences to prevent other organisms gaining a foot-hold.

14

Food Processing and Sanitation

Food processing is the set of methods and techniques used to transform raw ingredients into food for consumption by humans. Food processing often takes clean, harvested or slaughtered and butchered components and uses these to produce attractive and marketable food products. Similar process are used to produce animal feed. Following are common food processing techniques:

— Removal of unwanted outer layers, such as potato peeling or the skinning of Peaches
— Chopping or slicing, of which examples include potato chips, diced carrot, or candied peel.
— Mincing and macerating
— Liquefaction, such as to produce fruit juice
— Emulsification
— Cooking, such as boiling, broiling, frying, steaming or grilling
— Mixing
— Addition of gas such as air entrainment for bread or gasification of soft drinks

— Proofing

— spray drying

Food processing dates back to the prehistoric ages when crude processing incorporated slaughtering, various types of cooking, such as over fires, smoking, steaming, oven baking), fermenting, sun drying and preserving with salt. Foods preserved this way were a common part of warriors and sailor's diets up until the introduction of canned food. These crude processing techniques remained essentially the same until the advent of the industrial revolution. Modern food processing technology in the 19th and 20th century were largely developed to serve military needs.

Nicolas Appert developed a vacuum bottling process to supply troops in the French army with food, which would eventually lead to tinning and then canning by Peter Durand in 1810. Although initially expensive and somewhat hazardous due to lead used in the cans, canned goods would later become a staple around the world. Pasteurization, discovered by Louis Pasteur in 1862 was a significant advance in ensuring micro-biological safety of food..

In the 20th century, World War II, the space race and the developing consumer society in the developed world furthered the development of food processing with advances such as spray drying, juice concentrates, freeze drying and the introduction of artificial sweetners, colorants, and preservatives such as sodium benzoate and saccharine. In the late 20th century products such as dried instant soups, reconstituted fruits and juices, and self cooking meals such as MRE food ration were developed.

Benefits of Food Processing

Benefits of food processing includes toxin removal, preservation, improving flavour, easing marketing and distribution tasks, and increasing food consistency. In addition, it increases seasonal availability of many foods, enables transportation of delicate perishable foods across long distances, and makes many kinds of foodstuffs safe to eat by removing the microorganisms. Modern supermarkets would not be feasible without modern food processing techniques, long voyages would not be possible, and military campaigns would be significantly more difficult and costly to execute. Modern food processing also improves the quality of life for allergics, diabetics, and other people who cannot consume some common food elements. Food processing can also add extra nutrients.

Negative Points

Food processing can lower the nutritional value of some foods. Some preservatives added or created during processing such as nitrites or sulphites may cause adverse health effects on some consumers. In addition, high quality and hygiene standards must be maintained to ensure consumer safety and failures to maintain adequate standards can have serious health consequences. In general, fresh food that has not been processed other than by washing and simple kitchen preparation, may be expected to contain a higher propotion of naturally occuring vitamins, fibre and minerals than the equivalent product processed by the food industry. However fresh matereials are more liable to early spoilage and are often unsuited to long distance transportion from source to shelf.

Components of Food Processors

Modern food processors come in three basic sizes: full, compact, and mini. No matter what size they are, however, the basic components are the same: a motor, a bowl with a lid and feed tube, and a set of attachments. The motor is housed in the base of the appliance, and it is the heaviest part of the device. Full-size machines generally have larger, more powerful motors, and can weigh more than 20 lbs (9 kg). This weight has a utilitarian value: The heaviness of the base gives the appliance stability and ensures that it doesn't move around while the motor is running.

Though the first food processor bases were clad only in white, hard plastic, today they are available in a range of stylish colours and with metal and plastic finishes, ensuring that your appliance will fit in with your kitchen decor. From the motor, a shaft extends upward to power the attachments. The bowl, which is usually made of durable, transparent plastic, fits onto this shaft and locks into position. The lid, usually made of the same material, locks onto the top of the bowl; in many older models, engaging the locking mechanism turns on the motor, but newer models generally have an on/off switch or button.

The lid has a feed tube fitted with a plunger. You can insert food into the device through this feed tube, pushing it down with the plunger. Some models have wider and narrower feed tubes for use with larger and smaller food items. The size of the bowl varies according to the size of the machine:

— Full-size bowls generally have a capacity of 9 to 13 cups.

— Compact-size bowls can accommodate 5 to 7 cups.

— Mini-size bowls can fit 2 to 5 cups.

Some models come with large and small bowls for use with the same base. The attachments fit over the shaft inside the bowl. Standard attachments for a food processor are an S-shaped blade — also known as a sabatier blade — and shredding and slicing discs. The sabatier blade sits at the bottom of the bowl. It consists of two small, curved blades arranged on opposite sides of a central plastic pillar that fits onto the shaft inside the bowl. The blades of the sabatier are usually made of metal, but are sometimes made of hard plastic. You may find that metal blades are preferable because they retain their sharpness longer.

The shredding and slicing discs are made of metal and sit at the top of the bowl, over the shaft. You push food down the feed tube and it contacts the disc, at which point it is grated or sliced into the bowl. The holes on the shredding and slicing discs may yield fine, medium, or coarse bits of food. You can purchase these different versions of the discs separately if they are not included with your food processor. In addition to the standard attachments that came with your food processor, you can supplement your equipment and make your appliance more versatile by buying additional attachments.

Other common attachments include:

— *A dough blade*: This blade is made of plastic or metal and has straighter (less curved) paddles than the sabatier blade. You use this to make dough for bread and pizza.

— *An egg whip*: This attachment has two straight arms with large open paddles at the ends. You use this to beat egg whites and whipping cream, incorporating sufficient air to ensure a fluffy end product.

— *A julienne disc*: This piece has a row of protruding, short, sharp teeth. You use this to cut food into long, thin matchsticks.

— *A French fry disc*: This is similar to the julienne disc but yields larger, fatter pieces.

— *A citrus juicer*: This is a dome-shaped attachment that fits on top of the shaft and turns to squeeze the juice from oranges, grapefruits, lemons, limes, etc.

— *A non-citrus juicer*: This purees fruits and vegetables introduced into the feed tube, collecting the pulp in the middle and straining the juice into the bottom of the bowl.

You can also find a special container to hold all of the attachments in one place, and extra work bowls, which can be handy if you are making several things in the food processor and don't want to wash out the bowl between tasks. Also, some models have different-sized feed tubes and bowls that can be used with the same base. These can help you perform a range of tasks without having to buy two different appliances.

Selection of a Food Processor

If you entertain often, a food processor can be a lifesaver. Even if you're just cooking for your family, it can save time and let you combine several functions in one appliance. Following are some steps

1. Analyse your need for a food processor. If you prepare food for large amounts of people and would regularly use the slicing, shredding, chopping and other functions of a food processor, you may be a candidate for buying one.
2. Consider the capacity you need. A 2- or 7-c. bowl is likely to be big enough unless you usually make large quantities of food.
3. Decide whether you need any extra slicing or shredding discs. Most food processors are sufficient without extras, but you may want to add discs now or later.
4. Check special features such as mini bowls, feed chutes, number of speeds, pulsing function and whether blades are reversible.
5. Look for a juicing function if you're interested in making fruit or vegetable juices.
6. Check that the parts are dishwasher-safe. This saves cleanup time.

7. Read warranties carefully, and check on service options and replaceable parts.

Using Food Processor

The shredding disc quickly and efficiently grates common ingredients like cheese and carrots, and the slicing disc yields perfectly even slices of potatoes and apples in no time at all. You just push the food through the feed tube using the plunger. Chopping, grinding and pureeing involve a little more technique. Let's illustrate this by learning how to make fresh salsa using your processor. You know that fresh salsa contains vegetables such as tomatoes and hot chillies; it can also incorporate ingredients like scallions, garlic, and fresh coriander.

You might be tempted to just throw all your ingredients into the food processor and turn it on, but you'll end up with something more like gazpacho soup than salsa. It's better to work in stages, because the different ingredients in your salsa will have different textures: You want the chillies and garlic pureed so that their flavour is distributed evenly throughout; you want the scallions and coriander finely chopped but not pureed, so that small green pieces are visible; and you want your tomatoes in bite-sized chunks. To achieve this variation in size and texture, you're going to have to introduce the ingredients one or two at a time, processing them in turn.

Since the garlic and chilli need the most processing, let's start with them. Peel a clove of garlic, remove the stem from a hot chilli, and throw them in the bottom of your food processor bowl. Then turn it on. You'll see that the garlic and chilli quickly get chopped up, but if your bowl is large, you might find that they get thrown against the side, away from the blades. You will have to turn off the motor and scrape down the bowl, putting the food pieces nearer to the blades again. You will also find that adding a bit of liquid (a tablespoon of fresh lime juice, water or olive oil would be perfect for your salsa) will help ensure that food thrown against the side of the bowl drips back down to the bottom rather quickly.

You'll also find that using a pulse action—turning on the motor for one second, turning it off for one second, then turning it on again for one second—gives the food time to drip down near the blades. Pulsing is one of the most important food-processor techniques; it allows you to keep an eye on the texture of your food to ensure that you don't over-process it. After 10 to 15 one-second pulses, and several scrape-downs, your garlic and chilli should be pureed. Now let's add the scallion and coriander. Be sure that you wash all the vegetables well, and trim off the roots and ragged bits.

Take the plunger out of the feed tube, throw in a scallion and a small handful of coriander, replace the plunger, and use five one-second pulses to chop up the greens, scraping down the sides of the bowl halfway through. Now, the tomatoes. First, cut them in half lengthwise, then into quarters, and cut off the stem tip. Now feed the tomato chunks into the bowl through the feed tube (with the motor off), and process them with three or four one-second pulses. Voila! Easy salsa, beautifully prepared. Pour your masterpiece into a bowl, season with salt to taste, and grab some corn-chips!

Mixers

A mixer is a kitchen appliance intended for mixing, folding, beating, and whipping food ingredients. Mixers come in two major variations, hand mixers and stand mixers. A hand mixer, as the name implies, is a hand-held device. It typically consists of a handle mounted over a large enclosure containing the motor, which drives two beaters. The beaters are immersed in the food to be mixed. Hand mixers are often battery-powered.

A stand mixer is essentially the same as a hand mixer, but is mounted on a stand which bears the weight of the device. Stand mixers are larger and have more powerful motors than their hand-held counterparts. They generally have a special bowl that is locked in place while the mixer is operating. Heavy duty commercial models can have bowl capacities in excess of 100 quarts (95 L), but more typical home and commercial models are equipped with bowls of around 4 quarts (4 L).

A typical home stand mixer will include a wire whip for whipping creams and egg whites; a flat beater for mixing batters; and a dough hook for kneading. Mixers should not be confused with blenders. Blenders contain sharp blades and typically operate at higher speeds that chop, liquify, or otherwise break down larger food items. A mixer is a much slower device without blades.

Blenders

A blender is a kitchen appliance used to blend ingredients or puree food. The term typically refers to a stationary, upright electrical device, which is to be distinguished from a hand-powered or electric mixer that may be used for similar purposes. A typical blender is built around a vessel for the ingredients to be blended. At the top of the vessel is a cap to prevent ingredients from escaping when the blender is switched on. At the bottom is a blade assembly, typically removable for cleaning purposes. The bottom seal is most likely watertight. The vessel rests upon a base containing a motor (for turning the blade assembly) with controls on its surface.

Most modern blenders offer a number of possible speeds. In 1922, Stephen Poplawski invented the blender. Stephen Poplawski was the first to put a spinning blade at the bottom of a container. He used his appliance to make soda fountain drinks. In 1935, Fred Osius improved on Poplawski's idea and invented the famous Waring Blender.

Espresso

Espresso consumption has grown tremendously in the last decade or two. There are drive-through espresso shops in parking lots. Sometimes an espresso cart will just park on the sidewalk, like the hot-dog vendors in cities. People have been buying espresso machines for their homes, too. These machines are smaller than the commercial machines found in cafes, but they work on the same principles. If you go to a cafe or espresso bar and ask for an espresso, what you will get is a shot-sized glass holding a small amount of very strong coffee.

There are many different types of espresso drinks, including cappuccino, cafe latte and cafe mocha. All are made with one or more shots of espresso. A shot of espresso is made by forcing about 1.5 ounces of hot water through tightly packed, finely ground espresso coffee. If everything goes well, what comes out is a dark brown, slightly thick liquid with a small amount of crema (a foam, sort of like the head on a beer) on top. There are many variables in the process of making a shot of espresso. The temperature of the water, the pressure of the water, the fineness of the ground coffee and how tightly the coffee is packed are just a few.

The skilled espresso maker, or barista, controls all of these variables to produce a quality shot of espresso. Let's start with one of the most crucial variables: the coffee. Espresso coffee is a blend of several different types of coffee beans from different countries. The beans are roasted until they are dark and oily-looking.

To force the water through the coffee, the simplest espresso machines use pressure that comes from heating water inside a sealed vessel. These types of machines can be bought for around $50, and there's even one that is made especially to take on a camping trip. They all work on the same principle, so we'll take a look at one of the camping-style machines. In this type of machine, the coffee is packed into a funnel-shaped piece of metal that has a tube extending to the bottom of the reservoir. A few ounces of water are put into the reservoir and the top is screwed on.

When the water is heated over a fire, pressure builds inside the vessel, and the only way for it to escape is up the tube, through the coffee and out of the tube in the top. Since the end of the tube is under water, the pressure forces the hot water up through the tube. There are some disadvantages to a machine like this. The pressure in the system depends on the temperature of the water. The temperature required to build up enough pressure to force the water through the coffee might exceed the ideal brewing temperature.

Coffee Makers

A modern drip coffee maker is a surprisingly simple device. Manufacturers have had 25 years to hone their designs, so these coffee makers are pretty straightforward once you open them up. The heating element is an aluminum extrusion with two parts: a resistive heating element and a tube for water to flow through. The resistive heating element is simply a coiled wire, very similar to the filament of a light bulb or the element in an electric toaster, that gets hot when you run electricity through it. In a resistive element like this, the coil is embedded in a plaster to make it more rugged. The heating element has two jobs:

- When you first put the water in the coffee maker, the heating element boils it.

— Once the coffee is made, the heating element keeps the coffee warm.

The heating element presses directly against the underside of the warming plate, and a white, heat-conductive grease makes sure that the heat transfers efficiently to the plate. This grease, by the way, is extremely messy. You find this grease in all sorts of devices, including stereo amplifiers, power supplies — pretty much anything that has to dissipate heat. The coffee maker's switch turns power to the heating element on and off. To keep the heating element from overheating, there are three solid-state temperature sensors.

The device attached directly to the coil is the primary temperature sensor. When it detects the coil getting too hot, it cuts off the current. Then, when it cools down, it turns the coil back on. By cycling on and off like this, it keeps the coil at an even temperature. The other two devices appear to be thermal fuses. They simply cut power if they sense too high a temperature. They are there for safety reasons, in the event that the main sensor fails. One part that is not visible in this coffee maker is a one-way valve. This valve is either in the hole in the bucket or in the aluminum heating pipe.

If there were no one-way valve, then the boiling water would be just as likely to flow back into the bucket as to rise up the black tube. The one-way valve lets cold water into the aluminum tube, but forces the bubbles of boiling water to flow up the black tube. If you blow on the tube leading into this value, the valve should be open. If you inhale through the tube, the one-way valve should block any air.

TOASTERS

For lots of people, the toaster is a daily part of breakfast (and lunch and maybe even dinner). A toaster is a machine for toasting food such as sliced bread and bagels. Toasted bread is called toast. Other toastable products may be described as toaster pastry. A typical toaster uses infrared radiation to heat a piece of bread. The heat is usually produced by conducting electricity through nichrome wires (Joule heating).

The toasting process consists of reducing the bread's water content (originally ~35% of total weight), raising its temperature, and slightly charring and caramelising its surface. The caramelisation process is a chemical reaction in which the complex starch molecules break apart into simpler sugar molecules upon heating. That is why toast is usually sweeter than normal bread.

Toaster ovens perform toasting functions of a pop-up toaster, however, the heating elements are positioned horizontally. A toaster oven usually has a glass door and a pull out tray upon which the object to be toasted is placed. Because of its design, a toaster oven can also perform some of the functions provided by a regular oven, but on a somewhat smaller scale. Toaster ovens are freestanding units, commonly placed on countertops or hung from cupboards (kitchen cabinets).

Refrigerators

A refrigerator (often shortened to fridge) or freezer is an electrical appliance that uses refrigeration to help preserve food. An industrial refrigerator or industrial freezer is simply a refrigerator used in an industrial setting, usually in a restaurant or supermarket. They may consist of either a cooling compartment only (a larger refrigerator) or a freezing compartment only (a freezer) or contain both. The dual compartment was introduced commercially by General Electric in 1939. Some refrigerators are now divided into four zones for the storage of different types of food:

— −18°C (0°F) (freezer)
— 0°C (32°F) (meats)
— 4°C (40°F) (refrigerator)

Features of Newer Refrigerators

— An LCD suggesting what types of food should be stored at what temperatures and the expiration date of the food stored.
— Filter Status Indicator tells you when it's time for a change.
— An in-door ice caddie, which relocates the icemaker storage to the freezer door and saves approximately 2 cubic feet (60 L) of usable freezer space. It is also removable, and helps to prevent icemaker clogging. In-door ice caddies are exclusive to side-by-side refrigerators.
— A cooling zone in the refrigerator door shelves. Air from the freezer section is diverted to the refrigerator door, helping to keep milk or juice in the door shelf colder.
— A power failure warning, alerting the user to the failure, usually by flashing the temperature display. The maximum temperature reached during the power failure may be displayed, along with information on whether the frozen food has defrosted or may contain harmful bacteria.
— Frost-free operation. Over time atmospheric water vapour condenses onto the cooling coils as ice, which can eventually build up into a layer several centimetres thick. This can be removed by emptying the refrigerator and turning it off so that the ice melts. In a refrigerator equipped for frost-free operation, a heater and a thermostat are fitted around the cooling coils. Every six hours (varies between 6 to 24 hours

depending on model) the cooling is switched off and the heater turned on until the temperature around the coils slightly exceeds the freezing point of water when normal cooling is restored. This melts any ice which has collected around the coils and prevents it from building up.

An increasingly important environmental concern is the disposal of old refrigerators—initially because of the freon coolant damaging the ozone layer, but as the older generation of refrigerators disappears it is the destruction of CFC-bearing insulation which causes concern. Modern refrigerators usually use a refrigerant called HFC-134a (1,2,2,2-tetrafluoroethane) instead of freon, which has no ozone layer depleting properties. Disposal of discarded refrigerators is very often strictly regulated by municipalities, by mandating the removal of doors, as many children playing hide-and-seek had been asphixyated while hiding inside a discarded refrigerator.

Basic Elements of a Refrigerator

The basic idea behind a refrigerator is very simple: It uses the evaporation of a liquid to absorb heat. You probably know that when you put water on your skin it makes you feel cool. As the water evaporates, it absorbs heat, creating that cool feeling. Rubbing alcohol feels even cooler because it evaporates at a lower temperature. The liquid, or refrigerant, used in a refrigerator evaporates at an extremely low temperature, so it can create freezing temperatures inside the refrigerator.

If you place your refrigerator's refrigerant on your skin, it will freeze your skin as it evaporates. There are five basic parts to any refrigerator:

— Compressor

— Heat-exchanging pipes—serpentine or coiled set of pipes outside the unit

— Expansion valve
— Heat-exchanging pipes—serpentine or coiled set of pipes inside the unit
— Refrigerant—liquid that evaporates inside the refrigerator to create the cold temperatures

Many industrial installations use pure ammonia as the refrigerant. Pure ammonia evaporates at -27 degrees Fahrenheit (-32 degrees Celsius).

Different Types of Refrigerator

— Freestanding
— Counter/cabinet depth: a refrigerator can be approximately 30 inches deep as opposed to approximately 35 inches deep like a normal refrigerator. This allows the unit to be more flush with surrounding cabinets.
— Built under: fridges and freezers which can be installed under the counter top.
— Integrated.
— In-Column fridges or freezers: these are built into a tall cabinet in your kitchen furniture. The appliance is built in to your kitchen so that it looks like a normal cupboard. Getting the right size fridge is very important when choosing integrated.

Door situation

— Eye level freezer refrigerator (or top mount).
— Bottom freezer refrigerator. The freezer is generally bigger and the refrigerator has two independent motor-compressors.
— French door (or trio). Similar to bottom freezer, but the refrigerator (top) section has two doors that swing outward like a kitchen pantry.

— Side-by-side. The unit is divided into two tall compartments, with the freezer on the left and the refrigerator on the right.
— Wide-by-side. Similar to side-by-side, but the refrigerator compartment is wider at eye level and becomes narrow at the bottom. Allows the convenience of a side-by-side, but able to fit wider items in the refrigerator.
— Single door. Originally, most units featured only one door, with the freezer compartment located within the larger refrigerator compartment.

Side-by-side refrigerators

The newest *side-by-side refrigerators* are the three-door models. Some have upper freezers that allow easy access to frequently used items with a minimal loss of cold air as well as lower freezers for long-term frozen food storage. For families that require a lot of refrigerator space, there are the separate refrigerator and freezer units designed to be used together. These units can be as large as 30 cubic feet each.

Built-in refrigerators

Built-in refrigerators and freezers are made to be flush with surrounding cabinets. To create the built-in look, custom panels can be placed on doors to match cabinets. Unlike top-mounted refrigerator/freezer models, which are about 30 inches deep, built-ins are only 24 inches deep. Some of the built-in refrigerator/freezers are taller, as much as 19 inches higher than top-mounted refrigerator/freezers, and they are 5 inches wider.

Pull-down door or access door models

Pull-down door or access door models have small doors

in the refrigerator that allow access to shelves inside the refrigerator. Frequently used items can be stored on those shelves and energy can be saved by opening only the small doors rather than the full refrigerator doors.

Defrost systems

With manual-defrost systems, the removal of frost and condensation from both the fresh food and freezer compartments are entirely manual. In partial automatic or cycle defrost systems, only the fresh food compartment is defrosted automatically. The freezer compartment must be emptied and manually defrosted. In automatic or no-frost systems, frost is removed automatically in both the refrigerator and freezer compartments.

Efficiency

The efficiency of a refrigerator is an important consideration because it uses more energy than any other appliance in the kitchen. The total cost of a refrigerator is a combination of the purchase price and what it costs to operate and maintain over its lifetime. High-efficiency models may carry a higher price tag but they may pay for themselves with lower operating costs. Operating costs depend on the efficiency of the condenser and motor, the type and amount of insulation, additional design features, and the daily use of the refrigerator such as the number of door openings per month.

Larger models and those with ice makers generally use more electricity. Models with automatic defrost systems use more electricity than those with partial or manual defrost. A manual defrost unit can use considerable energy if frost is allowed to build up over inch. The bright-yellow energy guide labels displayed on the fronts of appliances in stores can be helpful when comparing energy costs of different refrigerators.

The label will give the certified cubic foot volume, average annual energy consumption in kilowatt hours, and average annual cost of operation in dollars and cents. The costs vary from model to model along with the capacities, freezer sizes, temperature settings, and type of defrost systems. Make sure to compare units of the same size and with the same features.

Absorption Refrigerator

The absorption refrigerator is a refrigerator that utilises a heat source to provide the energy needed to drive the cooling system rather than being dependent on electricity to run a compressor. These refrigerators are popular where electricity is unreliable, costly, or unavailable. In the developing world gas absorption refrigerators running on kerosene are very valuable where there is no reliable electricity supply. Besides the obvious advantages for food preservation, they supply safe storage of vaccines and drugs.

In the developed world, including the United States, absorption refrigerators are most often used for camping and in recreational vehicles, though some are used in remote areas or in off grid homes. The heat source that powers the refrigeration cycle is most often a propane burner, though other fuel gases such as butane and natural gas are sometimes used instead in areas where these are more readily available.

Electricity can provide the heat for an absorption refrigerator and many camping versions can be switched to use it. In extremely remote areas, kerosene is used. The cooling components of absorption refrigerators can be constructed without moving parts and with no reliance on electricity. However, most new units have thermostats, ignition systems, safety pilot controls, and lights that introduce some moving parts and reliance on a nominal amount of electricity — little enough to be supplied by a dry cell or battery.

These refrigerators have the disadvantage of using a lethal gas, ammonia, although it is contained within a closed system; and if they are being run using an open flame then attention has to be paid to its safety and to maintaining the flame at an appropriate size. The basic principle of how these refrigerators cool their interior is the same as in conventional compression refrigerators. Both use refrigerant liquids that boil at low temperatures to achieve cooling. A large amount of energy is needed to turn the liquid into gas, and this is absorbed from the surroundings, cooling them.

The difference is in how the gas is turned back to liquid to use it again for more cooling. A conventional electric refrigerator uses a pump to compress the gas back to liquid, a gas absorption refrigerator uses another liquid to absorb the gas and then has extra stages to separate the pure refrigerant liquid out again for re-use, this extra part being where the heat source is involved. Variations exist, but the usual pattern of gas absorption refrigerator uses ammonia as the refrigerant and water as the absorber, with hydrogen gas included to adjust the pressure in the system. The exact mixture and pressure has to be correct to give proper cooling at normal temperatures.

The cooling system consists of four main parts: the evaporator, absorber, generator and condenser. The evaporator is where chilling happens as the liquid ammonia evaporates, absorbing heat from its surroundings to enable the liquid to turn to gas. The ammonia gas passes on to the absorber, where it dissolves in water. The solution flows down to the generator where the external heat source is used to bubble the ammonia out again. This gas is purified by condensing out water vapour before rising to the main condenser.

The condenser has big fins on the outside which let air cool it sufficiently for the ammonia to flow out of the bottom as a liquid again, down into the evaporator. The hydrogen plays an interesting part in making this cycle work. Why does the ammonia which turned to liquid in the condenser then evaporate at essentially the same temperature and pressure in the evaporator? Because the evaporator also contains hydrogen gas, and the partial pressures exerted by the two gases mean that the ammonia liquid will evaporate.

The hydrogen is present in the absorber too, but is not absorbed as it does not dissolve in the water. The ammonia, water and hydrogen system is closed. The water in the absorber is actually a weak solution of ammonia carried out of the generator when the ammonia bubbles out by a "bubble pump" like the pipe of a coffee percolator. There is no other pump in the system, liquids flowing back down under gravity and the gas pressure being the same throughout the system.

There are other gas absorption refrigerators which use only ammonia and water with a heat source applied intermittently, possibly just once a day. These have a pressure valve between the condenser and evaporator so that the generator and condenser are pressurised when the generator is heated. The liquid ammonia is forced slowly through the valve from the high pressure side into the evaporator where it evaporates in the lower pressure.

The pressure differential will last for some time after the heat source is removed, so active cooling occurs for longer than the time the heat is applied. When the pressures have equalised, the ammonia solution from the absorber can flow back into the generator ready for the cycle to start again. Gas absorption cooling principles can be applied at other temperatures, notably for air-conditioning where water may be the refrigerant, evaporated at low pressure and absorbed into a salt solution.

Food Sanitation Management

Food Sanitation is protection from contamination. All food products must be protected from contamination from receiving through distribution. Sanitation is a dynamic and ongoing function and cannot be sporadic or something that can be turned on once a day, once a week, etc.

Sanitation of Water

Water is essential in food preparation. It is used to wash food before cooking, it is used to act as a cooking medium, it is used to clean the containers of food before and after preparation and it is used also as the most important beverage Therefore, it is essential that all water meant for drinking and cooking purposes should be free from pathogenic bacteria. Water used for making ice must also be potable. The ice may be used to cool foods or added to cold drinks. Thus it is important to ensure that the ice we sometimes buy be made from potable water. Some of the diseases, which can be spread by the use of contaminated water, are cholera, typhoid, paratyphoid, bacillary dysentery and amoebic dysentery.

Sanitation of Equipment

It is necessary that all equipment coming in contact with food be kept clean. This includes knives, meat mincers, blenders, rolling pins, wooden boards, metal and porcelain dishes, utensils, etc. They should be scrubbed, cleaned with detergent and water and then rinsed with potable water. It is a good practice to see that such equipment are dipped in hot water at 80°C for at least 30 seconds or more and then allowed to drain dry. This sanitary step is especially important during epidemics such as infective hepatitis, cholera, etc.

Parts of blenders, mixers, etc., should be inspected after cleaning to ensure that there is no food material left over. If allowed to remain they could allow harmful microorganisms to grow and spoil the food. Equipment made of plastic and other such material which cannot withstand high temperatures need not be given the dip in hot water but should be given the other treatments and then allowed to drain dry.

In villages it is a common practice to scrub utensils and dishes with ash and then rinse them with water. The utensils and dishes are then allowed to dry in the sun. The alkaline ash acts as a good agent for killing any microorganisms adhering to the utensils and a sanitary effect is produced by drying in the sun both because of heat and the ultraviolet rays.

Insects Control

One of the common insects contaminating foods is the housefly. These have minute hair on their legs and thus can be the carriers of harmful bacteria depending on where they come from. It is possible that they may carry faecal matter or other such sources of pathogenic bacteria and deposit it on the food. Another insect, which can also be a source of contamination in the same way as the housefly, is the cockroach. These insects, which usually prefer darkness, have been known to cause diarrhea and dysentery.

Apart from these two common ones, there are innumerable insects ranging from the larvae found in wheat and rice to locusts, which can cause serious damage to food. Rodents, which include rats, mice and bandicoots, not only consume large quantities of food, thus contributing to the overall shortage of food in the country, but may also be the carriers of diseases such as plague. The presence of insects, insect fragments, rodent excreta and other matter of insect and rodent origin is aesthetically resented by consumers.

Health authorities condemn such food as unfit for consumption because it indicates poor practices of sanitation where the food was prepared. It is thus essential that preventive measures be taken to exclude the entry of insects and rodents in the house, especially in the cooking and serving areas. This can be done by:

— Keeping the prepared food in cupboards with wire-netting,

— Filling cracks, fissures in the walls and flooring which are usually the places where insects breed and multiply.

— Covering drains, holes, etc., with wire gauze so as to prevent the entry of rodents.

Precautions such as these if taken in villages and small towns where people normally stay in independent homes would certainly prevent the entry of insects and rodents. In large cities, however, where each building may have many apartments, unless measures are taken by the whole community, there is always a danger of insects and rodents travelling from one apartment to another. The control of insects and rodents can be carried oat in several ways of which the most common one practised in the home is spraying or dusting with an insecticide.

Fumigation may be resolved to in large godowns, factories, etc., as it destroys insects and rodents. Sprays or dustings make use of chlorinated hydrocarbons (such as DDT, TDE, aldrin, dieldrin, etc.) and the organic phosphorus compounds (such as Parathion, Malathion, Systrex, etc.) as the active ingredient for killing the insect. Baits in which chemicals may be mixed with food are also successful in getting rid of pests. Examples of these are

"Tygon" in which a chemical is mixed with sugar and a home-made mixture of boric powder and bengalgram dal flour, which when ingested by cockroaches results in their death.

Warfrain may be mixed with food and used as a bait for the elimination of rodents. It must be noted that insecticides are poisonous, and must be used in very small amounts only where needed. If used indiscriminately these are likely to enter our bodies and harm us after a period of time. It is important to store these out of reach of children and away from food, to prevent accidents.

Sanitation Tips

The first part of sanitation involves your own personal hygiene:

— Don't handle food when you are sick.

— Cover cuts, burns, sores, and abrasions with a tight, dry, antiseptic bandage.

— Shower or bathe daily when you are handling food.

— Keep your clothes clean; wear an apron and change it if you wipe your hands on it or it becomes soiled.

— Keep your hair clean and tied back.

— Use soap and plenty of hot water to wash your hands frequently, especially after any act that might contaminate foods.

Touching your eyes, mouth, ears, nose or hair, smoking, eating or drinking, using the rest room, sneezing or coughing, using a tissue or handkerchief, handling raw food (such as unwashed fruits or vegetables or uncooked meat), taking out the trash, touching a pet or animal, or touching any dirty surfaces (such as wash cloths, money or credit cards, or soiled dishes or linen). If you wear food handler gloves, throw them away after each use, or wash your gloved hands as thoroughly as you would wash your bare hands. Gloves can spread germs just as easily as bare hands.

As you prepare food:

— Keep raw food away from ready-to-eat or cooked food.

— Keep all food away from chemicals.

— Keep cold or frozen foods out of the refrigerator or freezer for as short a time as possible.

— Wash all raw fruits and vegetables before preparation.

— Cover food during preparation.

— When plating food, avoid handling tableware that may touch people's mouths.

— Never plate food that has touched the floor, unwashed hands, or dirty equipment.

— Always use tongs or scoops when necessary. Wear latex gloves, and never touch prepared food with your hands.

— Wipe up spills promptly.

— Hold food at proper temperatures. Some safe holding temperatures for food are:

— Stuffed meats and reheated leftovers: 165 degrees Fahrenheit (74 degrees Celsius) or above

— Cold food: 40 degrees Fahrenheit (4 degrees Celsius) or below

— Beef and other hot food: 140 degrees Fahrenheit (60 degrees Celsius) or above

— Fish and poultry: 145 degrees Fahrenheit (63 degrees Celsius) or above

— Cooked pork, pork products, hamburgers, and eggs: 155 degrees Fahrenheit (68 degrees Celsius)

Clean and sanitise equipment and utensils after each changed use. This includes knives, cutting boards, and thermometers. Storing food properly is also important:

— Do not refreeze food after it has thawed.

— Always label and date leftovers

— Store raw or thawing meats on the lowest refrigerator shelves

— Store shellfish in the original containers

— Always store food in food-grade containers and food wrap

Most harmful germs thrive in temperatures between 40 and 140 degrees Fahrenheit (4 and 60 degrees Celsius). This is known as the Temperature Danger Zone. However, that number may vary slightly as different health departments vary that amount by plus or minus 5 degrees. When you prepare food, keep it out of the Temperature Danger Zone as much as possible. Note that the Temperature Danger Zone includes room temperature. Whenever a potentially hazardous food (fish, beef, poultry, eggs, dairy products, shellfish, pork, some beans) has been in the Temperature Danger Zone for four hours or more, it should be thrown out.

Salmonella bacteria are the number one cause of foodborne infection in the United States. Typical sources of salmonella are meat, poultry, and eggs. Infection can be prevented by cooking food thoroughly and chilling leftovers rapidly. There are two special methods that can help raise the standards of sanitation in your kitchen. The first is the two-spoon tasting method. Use a clean spoon to scoop up the item you wish to taste. Pour that food into a second clean spoon and then taste it.

Never taste food over an open container. This ensures that the spoon you taste from does not go back into the food you are preparing. The second method is also one of the most effective ways of preventing the spread of germs: hand washing. Wet your hands with hot water and wash your hands and wrists with soap for at least 20 seconds. Scrub your nails with a nail brush. Rinse your hands with hot water for 20 seconds. Follow this procedure twice after using the restroom.

Dry your hands using a single-use paper towel or an air dryer. Kitchen towels can retain germs. The methods you use for thawing food is also an integral part of safe food handling. There are three safe ways of thawing frozen food: in a refrigerator, under running water, and in a microwave. Never thaw frozen food at room temperature. It runs the risk of contamination whenever it is left at room temperature. When thawing frozen food in the refrigerator, remove the food from the freezer. Thaw only the amount of food you need.

Place the wrapped food in a shallow container on the lowest shelf of the refrigerator. Do not unwrap the food for thawing. Make sure the refrigerator temperature is cold enough to keep the thawing food cooler than 40 degrees Fahrenheit (4 degrees Celsius). Leave the food in the refrigerator until it is totally thawed. Large amounts of food or food in boxes can take several days to fully thaw in the refrigerator. When thawing frozen foods under running water, begin by removing only the amount of food you need from the freezer.

Make sure the food is tightly wrapped or placed in a watertight container. Place the wrapped food or container under cold running water of 70 degrees Fahrenheit (21 degrees Celsius) or less. Make sure the water doesn't directly touch the food and that the food doesn't directly touch the sink. Leave the food under running water until it is completely thawed. When thawing frozen food in a microwave oven, begin by removing only the amount of food you need from the freezer. Put the food in a microwave-safe container.

Adjust the microwave setting according to the manufacturer's instructions. Start the microwave. Thaw food in a microwave oven only in emergencies. Cook food immediately after microwave thawing. Microwave cooking causes food to lose moisture and reduces its quality.

Sanitation Programmes

The primary rule of sanitation is to pay strict attention to food temperatures.

— Avoid prolonged holding in the danger zone.

— Provide functional thermometers to all food storage boxes.

— Monitor the temperature on serving lines on a regular frequency.

— Thaw frozen foods under refrigeration or under cold water.

— Do not thaw foods at room temperature.

Personnel Training

Regardless of type of processing or food handling operation, the number one consideration in food sanitation is people. It is people who set the rules, follow the rules, and also break the rules of sanitation. A sanitation programme is as good as the attitude, willingness, and efforts of people. That is why the most important aspect of a sanitation programme is ongoing personnel training. It is essential that the full meaning of sanitation and its wide economic scope be accepted by everyone concerned in the food system-including management. Personnel training should include appropriate sanitation principles and food handling practices, manufacturing controls, and personal hygiene practices.

Sanitation Principles

Personnel training should instill and nurture an understanding of the processing steps and technologies for each product manufactured or handled and where potential problems exist, and create a keen desire to satisfy and guard the consumers' interests. Production personnel must be trained in the critical elements of the operations for which they are responsible, in the importance of these operations, monitoring these operations, and in action to be taken when these operations are not controlled. Certain industries have developed certification programmes for operators of essential heat-processing equipment. If such programmes don't exist for a given processing segment, it is important that specific training programmes be developed for such personnel.

Hygienic Practices

Communicable diseases

Persons known to be suffering from, or known to be carriers of a disease likely to be transmitted through food, must be restricted from any food-handling area. Likewise, persons afflicted with infected wounds, skin infections, sores, etc., must also be restricted from these areas. Any persons with open cuts or wounds should not handle food unless the injury is completely protected by a secure, waterproof covering.

Hand-washing

Facilities with hot water for hand-washing must be provided and must be convenient to food handling areas. All personnel involved in food handling must thoroughly wash hands with soap under warm-running, potable water. Hands must also be washed after handling contaminated materials and after using toilet facilities.

Where required, employees must use disinfectant hand dips.

Personal cleanliness

— Personal cleanliness must be maintained while involved in food handling operations:
— Sanitary protective clothing, hair covering, and footwear must be worn and maintained in a clean, sanitary manner.
— Gloves, if worn, must be clean and sanitary.
— All food-handling personnel must remove objects from their person which may fall into or contaminate the food product.
— Tobacco, gum, and food are not permitted in food-handling areas.

Personnel and visitor access to specific food-product handling areas must be restricted. Personnel involved in raw product handling must not be allowed in processing or finished product areas. Foot baths and hand dips, where required, must be properly maintained and used. Colour coding of clothing, maintenance and other equipment should be used to clearly identify raw vs. processed product operations.

Surroundings

Outside surroundings should be evaluated for sources of contamination such as vermin, bird harborage areas, drainage problems, odor problems, debris, refuse, and pollution-smoke, dust, other contaminants. Appropriate steps must be taken to contain and control any potential sources of contamination.

The two most important overall elements of any food-processing and -handling facility is that it should be cleanable, and so designed and constructed that it prevents entrance or harborage of pests or other sources of contamination. Unfortunately, many existing facilities do not readily meet these essential elements. The facility should have floors, walls, and ceilings constructed of suitable, approved materials which are durable, smooth, impervious and easily cleaned.

Walls should be light coloured and well-joined, and floors should be adequately sloped for drainage to trapped outlets. Openings to outside and/or non-food-processing or -handling rooms or facilities must be sealed. Instrument panels should be appropriately locked and sealed to prevent harborage of insects. Windows and doors must be tight and close-fitting. And doors in food-processing areas self-closing. Overhead structures should be situated and constructed to prevent contamination of the food products, and lighting is to be adequate with properly sealed, safety type overhead fixtures.

Heating, Ventilation, and Air Conditioning (HVAC)

Systems must be designed and installed to prevent build-up of heat, steam, condensation, or dust, and to remove contaminated air. Positive air pressure is required in microbiologically sensitive areas. HVAC systems should be designed to be cleanable, and air intakes located to prevent intake of contaminated air. Appropriate traps and vents are to be used throughout. There should be no potential of cross connections existing between human waste effluent and other wastes in the plant. Appropriate vacuum breakers or air breaks must be used.

Waste containers

Facilities designed to prevent contamination should provide for the sanitary storage of waste and inedible material prior to their removal from plant or surroundings.

Waste containers are to be clearly identified. In general, the facilities and various non-product contact surfaces and equipment must be evaluated to assess potential for food-product contamination. Shielding from overhead contamination should be provided as deemed necessary. Examples include: shielding over food product fillers or bottle conveyers, shielding from refrigeration unit drip in coolers, sneeze guards on food service serving lines, etc.

A well-designed food-processing or -handling facility is constructed to minimise traffic to prevent contamination. It is desirable to have a product flow-through that physically and operationally separates raw product functions from processing functions and finished product functions in order to avoid cross-contamination. Boiler and engineering rooms must always be separated from food-processing and -handling areas.

Sanitary facilities

Self-closing doors must be provided for all washroom facilities. Washrooms, lunchrooms, and change rooms must be separate from-and not directly entered from-food-processing and -handling areas. Such facilities are to be properly ventilated and maintained. Sufficient numbers of handwashing sinks, with hot and cold potable water, soap, sanitary hand drying supplies or devices, must be provided in washrooms.

A sufficiency of suitably located handwashing sinks are also necessary in food processing and handling areas. Hand-washing sinks should be separate from sinks used for equipment cleaning and other operations. A potable water, steam, and ice supply is imperative for sanitary food-processing and handling. Compliance with appropriate regulations and standards must be verified through testing programmes. Water treatments, if applied, must be maintained. Adequate water temperatures and pressures are to be provided in processing areas.

All elements and operations involved with receiving and storage of ingredients, packaging material, and other incoming materials must be evaluated and monitored to prevent potential contamination of the food product manufactured. Incoming materials must be received into an area which is separated from processing areas. Only safe, approved food-grade direct and indirect additives andingredients shall be used. Packaging materials used must be safe and approved.

Storage Rooms

Where appropriate and applicable, the temperature and humidity of storage rooms for raw materials, ingredients, packaging materials, and food should be maintained and monitored. Foods returned from retail outlets must be clearly identified and stored in a designated area for appropriate disposition. Storage conditions need be such that the safety of the returned food is not compromised. Detergents, sanitisers, or other chemicals must be properly labelled, stored and used in a manner to prevent contamination of food, packaging materials, and food contact surfaces.

Chemicals must be stored in a dry, well-ventilated area which is separate from food handling areas. All food-processing and -handling rooms and other rooms must be maintained in a clean, sanitary manner. A major source of plant contamination is from custodial personnel and equipment. All custodial brushes and equipment must be in good repair as well as being clean and sanitary. The overall requirement for design of equipment for food-processing and -handling operations is that it be cleanable and maintained in such a manner as to prevent contamination. Food-contact surface equipment standards-of varying thoroughness- have been developed for segments of the food industry.

Installation of Equipment

It does little good to have equipment which is designed to be cleanable, but which is installed in such a manner or location as to preclude its cleanability. Adequate space must be provided within and around equipment, and equipment must be accessible for cleaning, sanitising, maintenance, and inspection. A sanitary operations facility has a preventive maintenance programme which monitors equipment maintenance procedures. Such a programme specifies necessary servicing intervals, replacement parts, etc. Protocols and calibration methods must be established for all equipment that could impact on food safety. These include:

— thermometers,

— pH meters,

— water activity meters,

— refrigeration controls,

— scales,

— recording thermometers,

— hygrometers, and other equipment.

All reagents used for monitoring and verification must be documented and stored properly. Appropriate monitors must be used. Thoroughly evaluate the effectiveness of cleaning and sanitising programmes. Consult a reputable cleaning and sanitising supplier and follow recommended procedures for cleaning and sanitising both food- product contact and non-product contact surfaces in specific operations. An adequate pest control programme is necessary for sanitary operation of a food-processing or -handling facility.

Effectiveness of the pest-control programme should be verified on a regular frequency. An important part of food sanitation programme is having a working product-recall system in place. The recall programme establishes procedures to be implemented in the event of a product recall. Written recall procedures should be established and tested for validity.